MESHA WILLIAMS

NOBODY'S SAVIOR

NOBODY'S SAVIOR

NOBODY'S SAVIOR

FROM TRYING TO SAVE THE WORLD, TO DOING MY PART

"YOU ARE CHOSEN, EVEN WHEN BROKEN"

- MADISON RYAN WARD

First published by MyHeight-MyCrown 2025

First edition

ISBN: 979-8-218-61185-9

CONTENTS

DEDICATION

I dedicate this book to myself. All of me. The part of me that tried to do something good, those parts of me that indulged in the bad, and the ugly parts that interfered with my growth. Everything I have gone through has brought me to this very moment of understanding that Jesus bled so I didn't have to. To God for our growing friendship that will continue to blossom! To those of you who were like me, trying to save the world, let's agree that we now know the truth about who's the one and only true Savior, Jesus Christ.

ACKNOWLEDGMENT

———————————

Give thanks.

To God for fertilizing the gifts he placed within me. For his unwavering love, guidance, and friendship. In his totality, I am made anew!

I thank my son for choosing me.

I am thankful to my dad for raising me.

I am grateful to my auntie Jennette for nurturing me.

I am forever grateful to my sister for being loyal to me.

I am thankful to my therapist, Lena Chapman, for aiding me and allowing me to process, unpack, and release.

To basketball for loving me, keeping me safe, and allowing me the confidence to have dominion over the gift God gave me.

Yes, basketball again for leaving me, because without its departure, I would have never understood the root cause of the cumbersome cape I carried for so long!

SAVIOR COMPLEX

"They said to the woman, we no longer believe just because of what you said; now we have heard for ourselves, and we know that this man is the Savior of the world," (John 4:42 NIV)

For as long as I can remember, this Savior complex has been a part of me; encouraging me to believe that somehow, I could save the world. Imagine that! Little old me becoming "MESHA ALMIGHTY," cleaning up the streets, laying down my life, and guiding my sheep! No ma'am. Not at all, but that didn't stop me from trying. The desire to be for others what I could not provide for myself, led me down a dark road, but eventually to the light! Are you like me? A person who can see greatness in everyone else except in oneself. If so, come with me on this journey as we unlock and transform our understanding of being a good Samaritan but "Nobody's Savior."

Growing up on the south side of Saint Louis and often moving around the city, poverty was the catalyst for this savior complex. I made it my duty to put my family on my back and get them out of the hood and on to a better life. This ambition was unbeknownst to them. The only thing my dad wanted for me was a college education. As an adolescent, I did not even understand we were poor; to me, it was normal. Everyone around me had the same means. Later, realizing my circumstances, I was determined to use the gift God gave me in sports to better my situation and those around me. Similar to Monica, from the 2000 classic movie "*Love and Basketball,*" played by the legendary actor Sanaa Lathan. Monica believed in her greatness and aimed to become the first girl in the NBA. Now, I know what you are thinking, in the paragraph above, I stated that I could only see the greatness in others. Let me explain.

Like Monica, after discovering basketball at the tender age of six, I believed I would be on my way to the NBA, and no one could stop me. Hanging on my bedroom wall was that iconic Michael Jordan poster. You know, the one with his arms stretched out, palming the ball, one in each hand. There had been hours spent sitting in my room aiming to recreate this image with multiple failed attempts, seeing that my hands were miniature. Basketball was the only thing that provided the confidence needed to catapult me and my family into another tax bracket, and that was the start! Savior, Savior, here I am!

This book will have examples of this "Savior Complex" behavior. I hope you will not judge me but see me. See my growth throughout my ebbs and flows, acknowledge the strength in my vulnerability, the unease of my quirkiness, and the intentional fight to heal. It is difficult to walk with Christ; in fact, it is the most strenuous thing I have done in my life, but it is WORTH IT!

THE FIXER MENTALITY

The aspiration to save my family from generational poverty was only the start of this savior complex. This idea manifested its way into relationships, work, and everyday life. To the point, it gave me a sense of satisfaction to be the one to help or at least try to extend aid to someone. In a way, this behavior later changed my good Samaritan heart posture into a self-seeking heart posture. I became "A Fixer." According to psychology, a "fixer" or a person who has a "fixer mentality" is someone who has a need to "save" others and thinks they know how to solve other people's problems. This act became a problem in most, if not all, of my relationships with men. This one guy, no I will not tell you what time in my life this happened, but trust me, it happened. This person let's just call him Jake, and no, not Jake from State Farm! Jake was an atheist. He was the type of "non-believer" who praised a "higher power" but never believed in Jesus Christ. You know what happened next; right? You guessed it, after trying to beat him into submission by periodically sending daily devotionals, suggesting worship songs, and trying to pray with him instead of for him. This relationship was going nowhere fast! Although there were other issues, this was a problem on my part, as if the good Lord needed my services. Here I am, a broken girl trying to aid another separated person. The nerve! Let me put it to you like this. He had a flat tire, and I was riding on a spare with little traction, fighting to save him. No, indeed! Jake needed to make the call for roadside assistance on his own because I could barely pick up the phone to dial them up for myself!

Okay, since you asked. Another example of me displaying these practices of trying to solve or help others' situations was in a work setting. I worked for a nonprofit company as a resource specialist. In my role, I provided and searched for tangible resources for clients. This kind of environment is a breeding ground for those of us, who feed off being the "captain saver." If there is any place on earth to do it; this would be it, right? Wrong! It was the first time a light bulb went off in my head, and I thought, "Can I really save the world?" To be honest with you, it never crossed my mind that I could not. From an early age, I had it all mapped out. The NBA by twenty-two, develop a clothing line for tall women by twenty-eight, and like Pinky and the Brain, take over and save the world! Another ongoing goal was to create generational wealth and open a nonprofit food pantry. In the beginning, I was so excited about this new job. This environment would be a place where one could nurture and support others. Savior, Savior, here I am!

During this time in my life, I was trying to change and become more interactive in work settings. I was the typical worker who said nothing, ate lunch in my car, only asked questions when needed, and was not much for small talk. I never trusted people or companies at all. Wait, stop thinking what you are thinking! You are asking, "Well, how can you desire to rescue people but not trust people?" That will take a minute to unpack. We will get to that a little later throughout the book. Stay with me.

In my experience, company meetings and team building retreats talked a good game about employees having a voice and encouraging us to speak up. They would even go as far as supplying a suggestion box to provide feedback on what they could do better. Sadly, most times, voicing your opinion was grounds for write-ups, suspensions, or in my case, TERMINATION. Let me explain.

While cultivating relationships with clients, extending resources to them, and then engaging in department meetings. It became clear that most of the concerns expressed by clients and co-workers still needed to be met. So, here I am! Like a moth to a flame, I was on it! I conveyed the perspectives of the community in meetings, assumed further responsibilities, and pointed out readily available solutions. Yet, with efforts averted, no actual change occurred. Their lack of urgency concluded; that I was right all along. They did not want to hear the genuine issues. They would continue putting bandages on the problems. The end of a workday was exhausting. Maybe because innately, I could deeply empathize with others. Some stories told by clients saddened me. Or could it have been because I saw myself in them, shattered to a thousand pieces? Quiet as kept, your girl was a paycheck away from being in the same position they were. Feeling helpless and taking that affliction home with me every night was daunting. Again, I asked, "Can I really save the world?" At that moment, I considered and realized three things. One, not everyone could receive help. Two, not everyone wants help, and three, my going silent is not the right action to take. Unfortunately, that is what happened. I was certain that the company could have made a greater impact on the community. In Hindsight, I understand that using government and private funding limits how companies can allocate funds. Even non-profits are about their business too!

After this consideration, the silence hit the fan. Subsequently, the war was over, at least in my mind. I retreated to being the quiet, no-question-asking worker I once was. Of course, this did not go over well. It became noticeable within the department that your girl was not the same enthusiastic worker she started out being. In my defense, my work did not falter, but my demeanor had. Frankly, I was over it and did not want to be there anymore, and it showed. If there was no way possible for me to do the things necessary to make actual changes, then my opinions in meetings were no longer needed in my eyes. Again, as stated before in the example with Jake, I will always acknowledge my tort, in a matter. In recognizing your mishaps in situations, there is an invitation for you to grow, and that I did!

One lesson learned from this ordeal was not to give up on getting what I considered justice for other people. Going into a shell, as I often did in times of conflict, only hindered the people I wanted to help. It prevented me from growing effectively and communicating with the opposition. It impeded my ability to summon the power to succor myself in times of despair. If I did not have the perseverance to fight for others, how could I fend for myself? Remember, everything in life is a reflection pointing back at you. This lesson also taught me the saying is true, "Not everyone wants help." Some are so used to being crushed that they are unsure how to cope outside of their dysfunction. There had been stories of clients who used the system as a crutch. However, this was not my experience, but we all know of someone whom we gave an inch, and they took a mile. The next lesson was not something unfamiliar to me, but something I had been facing throughout my existence. My fight with authority! For most of my life, I have been a rebellious person. A true "rebel without a cause." Not that I did not like authority. I just did not respect people who abused their position of power. In my life experiences, many people have mistreated their hierarchy in certain situations. So, to protect me, or at least what I thought was safeguarding my heart, the walls of Jericho did not fall, they stayed up!

The mind of a person with a "fixer mentality" is one of complexity and insecurity. Now, I am not a psychologist, so allow me to stick to telling you about my flaws and overview while functioning as a "fixer." People who have this behavior genuinely want to help other people. Unfortunately, somewhere along the way, the satisfaction gained when helping others surges and becomes a bit of a high. Aiding someone in need fed the lack of confidence in not feeling needed. For a long time, I tied my worth to sports. When you are a top-tier athlete, you are a hot commodity. Everyone wants the opportunity to be on your team, say they have the privilege of coaching you, and or, say they played against you. Not to toot my horn, but TOOT, TOOT, your girl was that player. Sadly, when the curtains closed, the roars stopped, and my dream of being the first woman in the NBA was gone! Who will need or want me now? It was a hard pill to swallow and trust for years; I was choking.

THE SAMARITAN WOMAN

"Go call your husband and come back. I have no hus-
band, she replied. Jesus said to her, you are right when you
say you have no husband. The fact is you have had five
husbands and the man you now have is not your hus-
band." (John: 4:16-18 NIV)

Now let us take a moment and read that scripture above one more time! In my earthly mind, that was a read! I for sure would have clutched my pearls if the good Lord told me something like that!

"The fact is you have had five husbands."

Whew! Not five! Okay, let a sister live. Do not act like your past is squeaky clean. Oh, and let me rephrase that. I have clutched my pearls on several occasions when he has checked me. But of course, if you know him, you understand he is meek and lowly at heart, and this was not a read but an invitation! Jesus met her where she was, despite the beef between the Jews and Samaritan people and regardless of her past. I enjoyed this chapter because, as a chronic "fixer," I did not need to wait until I stopped trying to fix others before seeking after him. He met me right in my messed-up situation. Every relationship I have had mirrored the shattered pieces of me. The Samaritan woman did not have five husbands, and an attainable sixth, because that's who she was. Just like the rest of us might do, the Samaritan woman looked for something in her husbands she could only find in living water! That living water is our one and true, Savior, Jesus Christ.

While continuing to read this chapter of the Bible, one of the most important things stood out to me. The Samaritan woman showed no signs of "clutching her pearls" or "being appalled" by Jesus making that statement to her. Instead of becoming defensive, she replied,

"Sir, I can see that you are a prophet." (John 4:19 NIV).

This response was telling of her. It did not seem like she was ashamed of her past or current situation, but eager to have whatever Jesus offered. Or for all we know she was at her breaking point and would do whatever she needed to get to a place of healing. Or maybe the Lord's presence provided her with the comfort she needed to take the first steps to a better life. Scripture says that she left her water jar behind and went back to the town to tell the people about a person who told her everything about her life. Maybe her leaving the water jar behind symbolizes her retiring from her past. What should you leave in your rearview to move forward in your walk? Is it a fixer like I was? (Still a work in progress.) Whatever it may be, know that you have the power within to break any chain or weapon that may try to form against you, if you have the

Holy Spirit guiding you. I am excited for you! Breakthroughs are coming!

The notion that I could fix everyone's problems was absurd. How could a person force someone into healing? Everyone has their journey and their own time, in which they will start the healing process. I now understand that this displayed "Savior" behavior was a trigger response to feeling rejected. The experienced rejection made me feel like I had something to prove. It catered to the craving desire of wanting to be needed. For instance, the first thing I had ever loved was the first thing that broke my heart. I know what you are thinking, some guy, right? Nope! The culprit was basketball. That's right; basketball was my first love! As mentioned, I fell in love with the game at the age of six and have been in love ever since. Well, until I found a new love for Christ after my baptism. We will talk about that a little later. Now, I may often reference the movie "*Love and Basketball*" because it is one of the best basketball movies ever, and I relate to the character Monica a lot. Okay, not a lot because I did not get the guy, which I am not mad about. No shade, but what is for you will be for you! Unless you happen to be in a situation like Saul was when he missed his turn to be King, because of his disobedience. Anyhow, I never went to the league or played overseas, but I got to play basketball at the semi-pro level. Nonetheless, we both had the same heart and love for the game, even the same attitude. We walked around with a chip on our shoulder with something to prove.

"I'm a ball player; if anyone knows what that means, it should be you,"

Said Monica's character as she was standing outside her dorm building. When she makes this statement, she is speaking to her boyfriend Quincy, played by another legendary actor Omar Epps. These were my sentiments exactly! After my basketball career ended, I found it hard to watch this movie, but when I did and repeated this line, I directed it toward basketball. How could the game I love so much, dedicated decades of hard work to, that awarded me such confidence and kept me safe, leave me? Basketball knew that it was all I had at the time! It knew that "I was a ball player," where would I be, or what would I do without it? It sounds like a horrible breakup, and it was! If not "Mesha, the tall girl who played basketball," then who was I? Unintentionally, I had wrapped my entire identity into the sport over the years, and it was over just like that! Thrust into the game with a goal and a fire to show myself as a dignitary but came out of it damaged and defeated. If I could not save my relationship with the one thing that had been close to my heart, finding someone who needed a "Savior" and redeeming my worth through them would be the next best option. So again, Savior, Savior, here I am!

Unfortunately, it was over a decade before I recovered from the hurt basketball caused me. It took therapy, the birth of my son, and a great deal of soul-searching to begin the healing process. The ultimate flex was when I became intentional about seeking an intimate connection with Jesus. Like the Samaritan woman, I had looked for value and the need to be longed for in all the wrong places. Soon, the notion that the birth of my son would be sufficient would diminish. When my child was born, he filled the void that basketball had left. My therapeutic sessions often revolved around the anxiety I felt about his impending departure. Like my sentiments with basketball, who would I be if my baby boy no longer needed me? Of course, he is only thirteen, but the mere fact he was finding independence away from me pierced my heart. During the pre-teen years, adolescents believe, as the song states, that "parents just don't understand"! Has God been trying to teach me this all along? That he is the only one who will never leave me or forsake me? God is the only one with the power to love you, build you up, chasten you, fill voids, and simultaneously bring you peace. The Bible says,

> *"For my thoughts are not your thoughts, nor are your ways my ways, says the Lord." (Isaiah 55:8 NIV).*

It is not that our family does not love us or can't help us in times of need, but they are only human. The only one with the ability to complete you is also the one that created you! I would soon realize that I inadvertently made the game of basketball and even my son, my Savior and idol. Perhaps that's why basketball did not work out. We all know that God is a jealous God, and he wants nothing before him! Or could it have been that it was not in the cards for me all along? This concept was something I often thought about. Maybe the game was only around to give me the strength I would desperately need for the abundant life God would later allow me to have. I remember a coach telling me that "I didn't fit in the program," and that was the sole reason I was not playing. This statement stuck with me for a long time. It left me often pondering about this declaration; what was wrong with me? Why didn't I fit in? Foolishly, I accepted this opinion, afraid that other people would concur with the notion that my skills were not good enough to play at the collegiate or professional level.

Thankfully, the woman I have grown into today knows that basketball did not work out, not because I wasn't qualified or skilled enough to play the game. I truly believe that going to the league was not my calling because it was God's way of protecting me. Protecting me from myself mostly. During this time, my insecurities were not suitable to take on the rigorous commentary of mainstream media. His shielding covered me from the expectations that others would place upon me. Now, I understand he was building me up, establishing character, perfecting my endurance, and thickening my skin to withstand negative comments and the sufferings that come with being a follower of Christ. Like the remark from the one who told me, "I didn't fit in." He didn't create me to fit in; with this stallion height, he handmade me to "Stand Out."

"Yet you, Lord, are our Father. We are the clay; you are the potter; we are all the work of your hand." (Isaiah 64:8 NIV)

If I had faced scrutiny, with my "fixer mentality" and insecurities, I would have crumbled under the pressure. Primarily from the stress of trying to keep what I had longed for. Could I have been in any position to put my family on my back and bring them out of poverty? Between me and you, if I had played in the league and received the things of my dreams during that time, I would not be alive writing to you today! The saying is true. "The world's rejection is God's protection."

At the end of "Love & Basketball," Monica receives what was for her! Throughout my thirty-seven years on this earth, I have not always agreed with God about where he positioned me at certain times. With maturity and understanding, I am now realizing that what God has for me is better than anything I could imagine! However, occasionally, my ego and desires can impede my understanding of this. We as believers must be open to doing the will of God, no matter if his will aligns with our desires or not. Scripture tells us in

(Psalms 37:4 NIV) to "Take delight in the Lord, and he will give you the desires of your heart."

This means if you keep God first and seek him, his presence will change your heart's desires and what you want will begin to look more like the plans that he has for you rather than the plans you have for yourself. So, even after we have cried, felt anger, or jaded about our situations, eventually what he wants prevails. There have been several times in my life when I had been stubborn and neglected to listen to him. There would be occasions where I would ask for discernment, and then God would give me the perfect opportunity to use sound judgment, and yep, you know what happened next! As the social media content creator, Ariel Fitz-Patrick would say in her skits "I will see for myself." That is precisely what I did! Take, for instance, the time I burned parts of my hair off. Let me explain!

The plan was to allow my hair to grow longer, to achieve a protective style known as box braids. This is where the impatience, the cheapness, or the lack of funds to achieve this hairstyle came into play. As a natural-haired girlie, my hair would not lay as flat as I would have liked, but I didn't want to cut it off again. Not to mention, at that time, my hair was platinum blonde, which is my favorite hair color! My recent hair growth had made its way through, and bleaching it was the only way to execute this signature look. So, like the song says, "making my way downtown walking fast faces pass and I'm home-bound." Back at the crib after a beauty supply run, with items in hand, I was ready to achieve this look! Oh, and as far as the song goes if you know, you know! Now, I am not a licensed cosmetologist, but I have been doing my hair for a while. We all know that you should not bleach your hair twice in one day. Since this was a normal routine for years, I did it anyway! Now do not judge me, I am sure you have some hair stories too! As if that was not good enough. I had another impulsive idea that leaped into my frontal lobe, and the next day a no-lye relaxer was applied to my hair! Look, I can feel the judgment as you are reading this! Let me live, okay? No need to tell what happened next, but as Jay-Z said, "Allow me to reintroduce myself," My name is Fire Marshall Bill! If you have ever seen the classic TV show "In Living Color," then you know the character I am speaking of. Fire Marshall Bill was a character played by the celebrated comedian, Jim Carrey. His character and I were twins. There were patches of my hair gone, and chemical burns were throughout my scalp. It was a mess that I caused but wait, there is more to the story!

Right before applying the relaxer, there was a commercial on Pandora that said, "If you have used a no-lye relaxer and it has given you cancer, please call this number." You all, I cannot make this stuff up! Understanding that this was a sign for me not to do what I was about to do, my comment aloud to God was "God, I know this is you talking, but I'm going to see for myself!" Talk about being disobedient!

Do you recall a time when you deliberately disobeyed your heavenly father? One thing I could not do at that moment was save my hair, so off it went! Shaved, almost bald. Savior, Savior, no I am not!

JOURNAL

A MOMENT TO RELEASE

The journal section below will be at the end of each chapter of this book so you can create a moment to release. Get comfortable sitting in the pain, discomfort, or even guilt you may be experiencing in your happy season. Yes. That is a natural emotion that people can feel. Process these emotions, unpack them, and then release them! Hand it all over to God! Here are a few questions to get you started. Feel free to write whatever is in your heart. There is no pressure to write anything if you are not ready! You have the right to unpack and release at your own pace.

Has God ever met you where you were? Has he shown himself to be gentle in his corrections? Give thanks and describe the details of your situation and how it made you feel to receive such a gift. Do you have a "fixer mentality"? If so, how has it affected your life and relationships?

A SAVIOR'S REJECTION

"You are my hiding place; you will protect me from trouble and surround me with songs of deliverance. Selah." (Psalms 32:7 NRSV)

Do you believe the saying "Rejection is God's Protection?" What if the rejection you feel comes from the one who created you? Let me explain. Growing up I believed myself to have been the underdog. Rejection after rejection, obstacle after obstacle, always feeling the need to prove myself. Not only to others, but to myself. Whether it be proving that I was talented enough to play basketball at a certain level, proving to be a rider for a guy, or even in platonic friendships. Feeling the need to perform for others became exhausting. If you are a fixer and you are in the same position, it is good for you, because a breakthrough is coming! On the brink of exhaustion, there is light at the end of the tunnel. As fixers, we sometimes bring this fatigue to ourselves. We want to be everything to everybody and leave our temples empty.

The ultimate breaking point, well one of my breaking points because I have had plenty throughout my years on this earth. This time, let us just say, was the final straw. This time, the culprit was a guy. Or all the guys and messed-up situations in my life that led up to this fellow. In this circumstance, the guy wanted all the benefits of being in a relationship but did not want an actual relationship. Back in the day, the old folks would say, "Why buy the cow when you get the whole milk for free?" Which means, why would a man or woman consider doing anything more for you when they can do nothing and still get what should be sacred? Most of us have been there before. In all my alliances with men, I mentally departed from the relationship, or as the young-ins like to call relationships nowadays "situation-ships," before I'd physically left. It was no different for this "situation-ship." There I go again, not paying attention to the warning signs, once again displaying my stubbornness. At this time in my life, if I am sincere, I believed in God but had not yet developed real intimacy with him. As we all know, believing in Jesus and having a deep and close bond with him are two different things. There were moments while in constant thought, I would think, "Girl, you have got to be crazy." Why are you still entertaining this guy? Stay with me. This is going somewhere.

As mentioned before, being raised by my dad and being his only child, the world would have you believe that girls who have their fathers in their lives have no "daddy issues," but I beg to differ. I'm not sure if my dad realized the expectations, he put on me as a young girl. Often, I felt as though he wanted a son instead of a daughter. It wasn't until one day in my mid-twenties as my father and a team of semi-pro teammates were eating at a BBQ joint in KC; that someone asked him "Did you want to try for a boy"? His reply was shocking, but a beautiful affirmation to hear. "NO, I got it right the first time," he said. If you could have seen my face at that moment, the joy I experienced in his words left me proud, grateful, and most importantly, seen!

Side note: Parents, if you learn anything from reading this book today, the words that you spew to your children, hurtful or uplifting, can have a major impact on their mental health. Be mindful of how you communicate. It's not always what you say, sometimes it's the delivery. Now that is not to say tiptoe around the truth. It is to say if you realize that you don't have the correct words or delivery in the moment, ask God to step in so that he can better abet you with your child. It is the trust between the child and the parent as well. Children need to know that they have a safe place to land their concerns. I include myself in this message.

Okay, now where was I? Oh yes, sometimes I would not feel good enough for him. Let me give you a little background on my dad, military-trained, God-fearing, a true "man's man," old school at heart, with a no-nonsense approach. Mesha, do this, this way, or Mesha, you are not doing this right. There would be times in my adolescence when I would lie about having homework to do so that he would not offer to help me. His tone and his teaching did not fit my timid personality. Please understand that this is no shade to my father. Trust me, we have had our heart-to-heart conversations, have grown closer, and are having an effective relationship these days! I love him to pieces and will always be his little tiger! Yes, tiger. He didn't call me princess. Your girl was too much of a tomboy for that, which was fine with me! Now, allow me to admit some woes that happened back then were not all his fault. The rebellious parts of me showed up often, and Mesha was going to do what Mesha wanted when she wanted. There was a time when in conflict with my son, God brought to my remembrance the strife I caused my dad, and I immediately picked up the phone to call him and apologize. It's funny how the tables turn, and the lessons your parents tried to instill in you have now passed along to your offspring. As I thought about the situation with my child, I knew my pops deserved the apology I had called to give him.

The situations above are examples of how young ladies, like the Samaritan woman, could seek validation from men in relationships. Was I seeking validity in these connections with men because of my daddy issues? I believe in certain instances; absolutely! Trying to prove to them, like Brandy, that I could be down no matter how they treated me. As I am writing this, though, I am uncertain that my insecurities and lack of self-worth all stemmed from the matters with my dad. Of course, other factors in my immediate surroundings supported the void I felt. The rigorous halls of middle school, the dysfunctional and abusive home I left to move in with my father, and the diaries of being a teenage girl. I'm sure it played a significant role as well. As children, once we develop into adults, it is our responsibility to seek the help and guidance we need to deal with the hurt or traumas we face as adolescents. We should not and cannot continue to blame our parents.

After the final straw incident with the one guy and a cumulative of all the guys, I had had it with doing things my way! In a deep conversation with a friend about how I felt depleted, I used the quote from Albert Einstein that said, "The definition of insanity is doing the same thing over and over, expecting different results." I had enough of doing things of my own accord. So, I thought. It is seldom that we stop our unhealthy habits after a revelation, but at least I was on the right train of thought.

Fast forward seven years had passed since I'd been walking with God and sadly, I had felt rejected by him. At this time, I believed nothing had changed in my life. My conversation with God went like this. "God, I have done everything you asked of me, and all the things I was supposed to do. Why haven't circumstances changed in my life?" There had been many stages I went through now that I was delivered. This phase was my routine stage. God was no longer my good-good father or my comforter, but he had become a routine. Through prayer and worship, Jesus revealed to me that I was manipulating his hand. After tithing, going to church every Sunday, in small groups, being intentional about reading my Bible, repenting of my old ways, and my constant pursuit of him. He showed me that my actions were the same as with basketball. I had put my worth into doing instead of being. It was like I was jumping up and down saying God, look at me, look at me! See God, I can be the daughter you want me to be. Look how much I am honoring you, Lord, and your word. Conclusively, these actions were still validation-seeking. This time not by some guy or some sporting activity, but by the one who created me! Now, you are thinking; Mesha, what is wrong with that? After all, he is your Abba, and he loves you. Yes, that is true, but as believers in Christ, we should know that we cannot outwork God. No amount of going to church, giving to the homeless, or sacrificing can make him love us any more than he already does.

"To obey is better than sacrifice, and to heed is better than that fat of rams." (1 Samuel 15:22 NIV)

His love for his children is unimaginable. We also need to understand that our worth is not tied to the work that we do, but to him and who he says we are.

"For we know, brothers and sisters loved by God, that he has chosen you." (1 Thessalonians 1:4 NIV)

My heart posture was wrong, but this does not mean that there was no rejection felt because indeed it was! It may have been delusional for me to think that seconds after being submerged in water during my baptism, my life would change for the better! Don't misunderstand, when someone commits themselves to Christ, they undergo a true restoration, but no one warns you that life will become darker before you can start to see the light.

After praying with my son before he went to bed, I would often go into the shower and weep. This time, as water flowed down the drain, also were tears of frustration and disappointment in God. I can still hear myself now, as the steaming hot water hits my back; "after all the rejection I've encountered, putting everything aside to seek you, I'm still invisible to you!"

Listen to me, sounding all entitled. Like God owes me something. At that moment, those were my exact feelings. Here I am Jesus, I said in a loud tone. Your word says,

"But seek first his kingdom and his righteousness, and all these things will be given to you as well" (Mathew 6:33 NIV)

and that is exactly what I am doing, Lord, chasing after you, I exclaimed, going down the list of accolades, feeling all accomplished. My discernment is up. I am in my word, fasting, giving, praying, and not for myself, but for others, and yet you still are not showing up in my life! To only have bits and pieces of you is not fair, Lord! At this moment, understanding the pain Jesus must have felt when he cried out to his father in **Matthew 27:46**, saying, *"My God, my God, why have you forsaken me?"* Looking back, of course, it was not to the same extent as what Jesus encountered, but there for sure was grief and betrayal that I experienced. It seemed as though nothing mattered, which made me feel inadequate to God. My feelings were very much hurt! So again, what do you do when you feel rejected and unseen by your creator, but in your heart, you know that you are already connected to the source, so there is no one else to turn to. What else is there for you to do? As a recovering fixer, the thought of taking matters into my own hands arose, but my years of self-work and pursuit of Jesus, afforded me the sense to know that I could not be like Usher and go back to doing things my way. So, as I continued sobbing and exclaiming; Savior, Savior, why have you forsaken me? I did the only thing one could do; I went to sleep. Before I laid my head on the pillow, I prayed that God would grant me the opportunity to wake up the next morning. Knowing that if he extended me that gift, then there was still a purpose and a reason to be on this earth. This notion brought a glimpse of hope into a desperate situation.

Months before this shower conversation with God, I sent my therapist a random text message. Shout out to her for reading, responding, and providing quality feedback. Below is the exact conversation that took place. Do not mind my grammar! I had to get it out!

THERAPY SESSION

6/26/22 10:57AM

Your thorn is your product and brand. What you struggle with and how you help yourself is what will help others. No it may never leave but it will encourage others. Profit off your thorn and help others.

The things I struggle with is also what I use to help others and that makes me human and relatable.

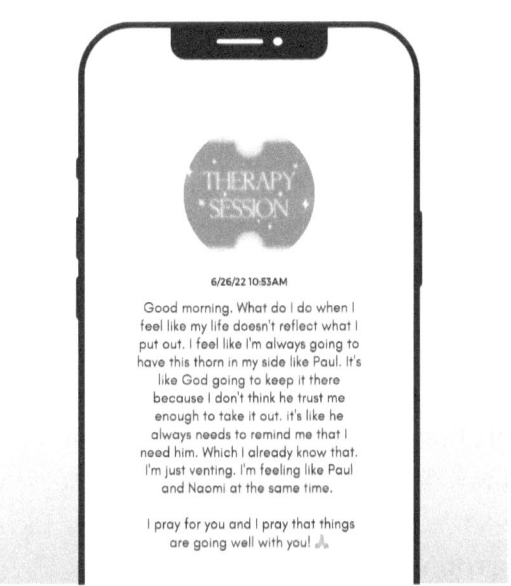

I am sharing this because it was the build-up to my shower conversation with God. When she replied and gave sound advice, it was the jolt I needed to keep striding and not give up on what God called me to do. In that instant of accepting what she said, I stopped worrying about tomorrow. Not that we should be living for tomorrow, because Scripture tells us in

(Matthew 6:34 NIV) "Therefore do not worry about to-morrow, for tomorrow will worry about itself. Each day has enough trouble of its own."

But what I mean is that when God graciously woke me up the next day, there laid the cross right beside me on my pillow! There was a choice to make that day and each day moving forward, whether to pick up that cross and walk with it, dying to my flesh or continue being spiritually dead. Honestly, when I sent the message to her, I had not read Paul's full story in 2 Corinthians. I just knew that there was a man in the Bible who had a thorn in his flesh, and that is what my trials felt like to me. After going back and reading the chapter, it confirmed my feelings and where I was in my season with Christ. It had seemed to me that from the time my lips uttered "I do" meaning accepting Jesus Christ as my Lord and Savior, my life had not changed much. Yes, I had the blood of Jesus covering me, and yes, I was repentant. Yes, I had been reading my Bible more than ever, but all the trials and valleys were still there. For the life of me, I could not figure out if it were something that I was doing wrong. Seven years of seeking, worshiping, and pleading with God for him to deliver me a life fit for an heir. The tribulations raised the question.

"What do you do when your life doesn't resemble what you know to be true about the calling God has for you?"

Again, your girl found herself stuck, just like at the end of my basketball career! Would it be another decade before coming out of this season? Would there be an answer from God on why I was going through so much turmoil? After reading and asking the Holy Spirit to help me understand his word, I knew that as a child of God, there would be no exemption from spiritual warfare. None of us are, but this season seemed like it was lasting forever! That brings me to one statement that had me shaken in that same text conversation with my therapist. Although she spoke life into me, she also sparked a dormant fear that lay within. She said, "It may never leave," referring to the thorn! Well, wait now what do you mean by "It may never leave"? My thoughts were like the lyrics from the iconic duo Outkast, from their hit song "Ms. Jackson" *FOREVER, EVER, FOREVER, EVER!*

Have you thought about that? That God is purposefully keeping his foot on your neck for you to remain close to him? It reminded me of the story in the Bible where God continued to harden Pharaoh's heart, which made him not let the Israelites out of Egypt. I remember thinking and asking God while reading the story, "If you want him to do what you wish, why do you keep hardening his heart"? It made little sense to me. It was the same for my situation. If God wanted me to be and do the things he called me to do, then why continue to keep this thorn in my flesh? My notion was God, how can I maneuver life in a slumped position and still be all that you created me to be? There were times I understood and was aware of what he was doing to better me. Then there were most times that I was entirely oblivious to his growing pains. However, he didn't need me to understand, but to have faith that even though I was facing challenges, I should trust that he is "King of Kings" and "Lord of Lords!" So, as we take a second to digest what we have just read, let's look at what Paul says in 2 Corinthians.

"Even if I should choose to boast, I would not be a fool, because I would be speaking the truth. But I refrain, so no one will think more of me than is warranted by what I do or say, or because of these surpassingly great revelations. Therefore, in order to keep me from becoming conceited, I was given a thorn in my flesh, a messenger of Satan to torment me. Three times I pleaded with the Lord to take it away from me." (2 Corinthians 12:6-8)

Now let us look at God's reply.

"My grace is sufficient for you, for my power is made perfect in weakness." (2 Corinthians 12:9 NIV)

After reading this, what are your convictions? Often, I questioned if God trusted me and the lack thereof was the reason for remaining in the wilderness. In my quest to figure out the wrongs in my walk with Christ, I had to question myself "Can he trust me?" Heck, "Do I trust me"? We have all heard the saying, "God gives you what he can trust you with." Had your girl been that untrustworthy, or was it just not my time yet? Maybe he wanted me to bake in the oven a little while longer. Or was this a just-in-case thorn? Paul stated in the verse above *"To prevent me from being arrogant."* This statement leads me to believe that this was a precaution to keep him right where the good Lord wanted him so that God's will could prevail! This could be the same as the previous example between Moses, Pharaoh, and the Israelite's. The hardening of Pharaoh's heart allowed God's promise to show the nations that he was the one and only true Savior!

In full transparency, I still have a thorn deep within my flesh. Your girl, as the title of this book states, is "Nobody's Savior." So, no, I do not have all the answers. Let me just say if you are going through this same situation of feeling as though your life does not resemble what you know to be true about what God has called you to do. I will tell you like the song says, "Hold on just a little while longer, hold on just a little while longer"! Here is a great scripture that shows you what and how to make it during this season.

"Finally, be strong in the Lord and in his mighty power. Put on the full armor of God, so that you can take your stand against the devil's schemes. For our struggle is not against flesh and blood, but against the rulers, against the authorities, against the powers of this dark world, and against the spiritual forces of evil in the heavenly realms. Therefore, put on the full armor of God, so that when the day of evil comes, you may be able to stand your ground, and after you have done everything, to stand. Stand firm then, with the belt of truth buckled around your waist, with the breastplate of righteousness in place, and with your feet fitted with the readiness that comes from the gospel of peace. In addition to all this, take up the shield of faith, with which you can extinguish all the flaming arrows of the evil one. Take the helmet of salvation and the sword of the Spirit, which is the word of God. And pray in the Spirit on all occasions with all kinds of prayers and requests. With this in mind, be alert and always keep on praying for all the Lord's people." (Ephesians 6:10-18 NIV)

I hope this helps you in whatever season you are in. God Bless you! Continue reading as I share more about myself and the why for writing this book!

JOURNAL

A MOMENT TO RELEASE

So, as I asked previously. What if the rejection you feel comes from the one who created you? Have you ever felt like this? If so, let's unpack and process these emotions. Unpack them and then release them! Hand it all over to God! Here are a few questions to get you started. Again, feel free to write whatever is in your heart. There is no pressure to write anything if you are not ready! You have the right to unpack and release at your own pace.

Talk about a time you felt rejected by God. How did it make you feel? Were you able to get over the hurt of the rejection you felt? Did God's rejection deter you from your walk to seek him? What was the outcome, and did you turn back to your "fixer" ways?

_____

_____

_____

_____

_____

_____

A SAVIOR TO NONE

"I have told you these things, so that in me you may have peace. In this world, you will have trouble. But take heart! I have overcome the world." (John 16:33 NIV)

It was amazing how God started revealing the unnecessary load I had attempted to take on my entire life. My struggles as an empath were also a major impetus in my savior complex behavior. At the start of this book, there was mention of my willingness to take on my family's burdens. Unwarranted, this was the start of it all. In God's timing, he enlightened me about my subconscious behaviors. With closer proximity through reading his word, the clearer my antennas of discernment peaked. This enabled me to see things about myself that I may have known but was in denial about or never knew existed. In the words of us millennial's, "I was today; years old!" When my light bulb began to flicker, highlighting my fixer mentality. Allow me to give you a little more background in my life before I tell you about my aha moment!

As earlier informed, growing up, basketball was the first thing I loved. It was getting closer to me going to college and your girl had a plethora of top Division 1 schools to choose from! That was until the schools saw my poor grades. After word got out, the Division 1 letters and calls stopped, and just like that, my life was imitating another scene from the classic movie "Love & Basketball". In this scene, Monica and her dad are sitting at the dining room table while her sister and mother prepare the table for dinner. Monica's father suggests she should start thinking about other options, because of her not being recruited, with it being so late in her senior year. Even though Monica and I were not considered for different reasons, and my father cared more about my education than sports. We were in the same predicament! After barely graduating from high school, I stepped on that JUCO campus with a chip on my shoulder and something to prove.

JUCO is short for Junior College. I ended up signing to Moberly Area Community College and played there for two years. Although going to Junior College was not in the plans, it was a wonderful experience! It was one of the top Junior Colleges around at the time. Like Drake, we went back-to-back making the NJCAA National Tournament but did not win the championship in both years. In my mind, I still envisioned heading to the NBA after college and then rescuing my family from the trenches. After graduating from Moberly, I then received another full-ride scholarship to Louisiana State University. Fast forward, after 2 SEC Championships and 2 Final Four appearances, the NBA nor WNBA were nowhere in sight, and things had not been going the way I had planned. My eligibility was up, and I had not received the playing time needed to be visible enough to make the WNBA draft. My dreams of going to the league were over! Depressed the entire time, and yet again struggling academically, it was hard trying to finish out my fifth year. Not to mention being pregnant! I was 7 months, with-child when I graduated from LSU and before giving birth became homeless, broken, and tired. The slight anxiety I feel writing this and thinking about this again is crazy. It is amazing how the body does not forget traumatic experiences. Anyhow, I am not sure if my homelessness added to my need to help any and every unfortunate person seen living on the street thereafter. I saw everyone in pain and in need as a reflection pointing back at me, and I felt compelled to save them! In hindsight, deep down, being their Savior would provide me with credence that I was worth saving as well! Aren't we all just mirroring each other? Seeing ourselves in others, not realizing when matters become challenging, we assume that opposition is often the problem, but we are just boxing with ourselves! That is not to say this is for every circumstance, because some opponents are just pure evil, but most of the time we are wrestling the person within.

Another favorite movie of mine is "Creed" starring Michael B. Jordan and Sylvester Stallone. Outstanding actor Michael B. Jordan plays a troubled young boxer, with a chip on his shoulder, in need of proving himself worthy of the family name, Creed! In one scene, Rocky Balboa, played by Sylvester Stallone, has Michael's character Adonis, standing in the mirror, sparring with himself. In boxing, this is called shadow boxing. Rocky tells him, "You see the person here staring back at you? That is your toughest opponent. Every time you get into the ring, that is who you are going against." That is what we all need to remember. We are our only competition.

"For we dare not make ourselves of the number or compare ourselves with some that commend themselves: but they measure themselves by themselves, and comparing themselves among themselves is not wise." (2 Corinthians 10:12 NIV)

Now for my aha moment! The instant God showed me about my fixer mentality was the start of him opening my eyes. I am not sure what I was doing or where I was coming from, but upon seeing this homeless person, there was an immediate sprint into savior mode, as usual. While contemplating what to give, the Holy Spirit spoke and said 'NO.' There was this strong feeling that I was not supposed to give him anything. Before this incident, I had never felt that way about giving to a homeless person. My "fixer" state of mind was always eager to help, but of course as a human being, it is always generous to support others in need, even if it is not much. It was the complete opposite when my pockets were full of lint! It was a horrible feeling not to be able to help them at all! The next time it happened; my cousin and I had walked out of this restaurant and there sat a guy on the window seal of a storefront with everything he owned holding a cup. Again, I heard; NO! The third time it happened, coming from church. Standing with his sign as his backpack laid at his feet, cup in hand, and just as I approached him at the roundabout; and quickly came the same NO as all the others. After these firm orders, there had to be a sit down with my Abba! My eyebrows raised in curiosity, and so I asked God one day while reading my

Bible. "Why can't I give to the homeless? Why are you telling me NO?!" Your girl needed to know! Low key, in my giving, is where I felt accomplished, in purpose, and of worth. I also wanted to know if it was me just thinking it or was the Holy Spirit really speaking to me. Guys, I cannot make this stuff up! While sitting in my prayer closet, I ask God these questions, and the Holy Spirit says, *"Because, you are nobody's Savior!"*

Let us just take a moment and appreciate how the good Lord got me together with five words! Okay, and now we are back! Now, to be clear, till this day, never have I ever heard God speak audibly. It is my belief that he communicates with me through people and through the Holy Spirit within me. It is often chills, uncontrollable crying, or thoughts that come so fast or brilliantly that I am convinced it was not my own. In this case, this correction was so fast it could not have been anybody else but him! Honey, he was quick and witty with the read, but of course, in all seriousness, he was just answering my question. His word says,

"Ask and it will be given to you; seek and you will find; knock and the door will be opened to you." (Matthew 7:7 NIV)

Without a doubt, he for sure came with the real! No lie, I was like, really, is that what we are doing, God! Okay. This is often my response every time he checks me. Either it is that sense of total dismay or tears of laughter. He has a great sense of humor, and through his correction that is how the name for this book came about! God gave it to me! Savior, Savior he is the one and only true Savior!

GOOD SAMARITAN, GONE WRONG

We always want more confirmation from God. So, clearly; his direct response was not enough for me for some reason, and again, "I had to see for myself." While pumping gas on a nice weather day in Dallas as I am inserting my card into the machine. From a far, there was a man who appeared as if he had nowhere to live. He had no shoes on his feet and looked as though he had not taken a bath in months. As I was waiting for the overpriced gas to fill my tank, boom, there came my fixer thoughts. Reviewing in my mind tangible items I could give to this man, all along knowing that I did not have a pot to piss in or a window to throw it out! This saying makes me laugh. The adages we heard our parents or elders say as adolescence cracks me up when I hear them. Anyhow, between you and me, I paid for the petrol inside my vehicle by over drafting on my bank card. Yep, your girl only had a dollar to her name sitting in the account. Talk about survival mode. I knew all the tricks to staying afloat until that next paycheck. All you needed was a dollar on your card, and instead of hitting debit when the machine asked for your 4-digit PIN, you would hit credit and type in your zip code. Boom! There you go! Experiencing nothing but gratefulness when seeing the machine's display read "Remove the nozzle and begin fueling." Okay, do not look at me all crossed-eyed like you have not done "I'm a survivor" things in your life. There is more to this story and plenty of other testimonies, and shady moments I could tell.

Continue reading to find out how the Good Samaritan moment turned wrong.

Maybe the phrase "turn wrong" is not the right term for what happened next. Let's just say the good Lord doubled down on his statement when he previously explained to me, I was "Nobody's Savior." While placing the fuel dispenser back into its place, the man seemed to disappear from my sight. Knowing that he could not have gotten far, I went to the trunk of my car to see if there were at least some old shoes or something for his feet. Locating my son's old pair of flip-flops, I got in my car, heading through the parking lot to cut him off in the direction last seen. There he was! Now this is no insult to any unfortunate person who is homeless, but normally the second you pull up next to them at an intersection and roll down your window, it is like a bat signal, they come running! Not this time. I rolled down my passenger window and even waved the flip-flops in the air to get his attention, and he just continued walking. In one last effort to heed the man my way, I said Sir, while waving the flip-flop again, but he just kept walking. Now granted, there had been a car in front of me waiting to get out of the parking lot and onto a busy street, but I was close enough for him to hear and see me. Not to mention, he looked like he had been on something, but because that had never been my experience with a homeless person before, I knew right then that it was God. He was confirming what he had been trying to tell me from the previous moments. That attempting to save them would not save me and the only true savior had already conquered the world! So, who was I to think that I could?

One day, months later, as I was scrolling on social media, there was a pastor who said: "You have to watch out for the chronic takers, but you also have to watch out for the chronic givers, too." That thing pulled my imaginary wig back! Was this who I had become? A chronic giver? So desperate to find myself that I inadvertently used my good Samaritan moments as an attempt to feed my soul! A lot of aha moments came to me in my prayer closet. While on the phone with my cousin, I revealed my belief that God was pointing out my selfishness. Let me explain. Have you ever received a call from someone informing you about a loved one's passing and instantly thought about your own demise? Or maybe you are the friend who only calls your bestie to talk about your problems, never giving them the opportunity to tell you theirs! Of course, yes, we are born into a sinful world, and like little children, we are so protective of what we think is ours. Not understanding that nothing is ours and our heavenly father provides everything that is given to us! We develop this selfishness through the world, yes, but it is also innately who we are as human beings. This is why the Bible tells us we must die to our flesh daily and

(Philippians 2:3 NIV) says "Do nothing out of selfish ambition or vain conceit, but in humility consider others better than yourselves."

Now, I never imagined myself to be an egocentric person until this incident. Sincerely, my heart's intentions began genuinely, just a young girl wanting better for her family and herself! Unfortunately, as life went on, I came across more disappointments, which further distorted my identity. Leaving me with a lack of knowing who I was and who's, I was! It led me down a bumpy road called "people pleasing."

"People Pleasing" breeds validation and affirmation from the wrong person might be a danger to one's self-esteem. In about my third therapy session, Mrs. Chapman gave it to me straight with no chaser, she said, and I quote "You are a people pleaser." What! No, not me! Say what, say, huh? I said, as she swiftly reiterated her statement, "Yes ma'am you are!" Sorry, but if you don't have a straight shooter as a therapist, then it may be time to find you another one! I'm just saying! I was sitting in my session in disbelief but also thinking in my head, "Yeah, she is right." Not only did I become a chronic giver, but I'd also become a "people pleaser" with rebellious tendencies. The war within continued to rage! The fight between my wanting true freedom and the urge to substantiate my worthiness reared its ugly head. There was a time when speaking to my heavenly father, I said to him, "God, I just want to be free"! His reply was, *"What does freedom look like to you?"*

Side note: When the good Lord asks you a question, trust that he already knows the answer. So, the question that he asks is not for him, it's for you. It's a question to see if you are aware of who you truly are.

My response was an exact definition of operating out of my flesh. Well, God, to me freedom is being able to move in this life how I see fit. Being financially free, traveling whenever and wherever, buying whatever, doing whatever at the exact moment I choose to. Not waiting around for someone to tell me I can, not asking an employer for time off or having to live paycheck to paycheck, etc. Going on and on, giving God my definition of freedom. Immediately after my rant, he says *"Oh, you don't want freedom, you want a lack of responsibility!"* After another yet jarring correction, I knew he was a thousand percent correct! I do not think that the things that I desired, God thought, were wrong. The issue was my heart posture. He is not so stern that he does not want us to enjoy the things that he created, but when your yearnings become bigger than your creator; watch out!

Not being sure where to go from there after his counter, he provided some help. A couple of months later, as I was sitting in the house of the Lord listening to Dr. Conway Edwards of One Community Church preach a series called "Why Marriage Matters." Even though his message was about marriage, the Holy Spirit still allowed his words to resonate with me when Pastor Conway stated,

"You don't get to have ultimate freedom if you do not have boundaries," - Dr. Conway Edwards.

That message hit me like a ton of bricks! Thereafter, I knew that redefining what true freedom meant would not come as what my flesh presumed it to be, but what the Kingdom of God said it to be. What I have learned so far in my walk with Christ and what that series taught me is that Jesus's love comes with boundaries. His boundaries are there to help you, not harm you. Being free is not without sacrifice, but most of all, being free takes faith, and true faith takes obedience. At the start of my walk with God, I was in awe. In this next chapter of my life, I want to still have reverential respect and fear, but also be in friendship, have obedience, and have unwavering faith and love for the God that I serve! The type of faith I speak of is the kind that the woman with the issue of blood had starting in *Mark 5:25*.

"If I just touch his clothes, I will be healed." (Mark 5: 28 NIV.)

Notice that she did not say if I just talk to Jesus or if he touches me; I will be healed. She was firm in her faith that if she were just able to get close enough, she would be healed, and like the hilarious comedian Kerwin Claiborne says, "And was"!

"Immediately her bleeding stopped, and she felt in her body that she was freed from her suffering." (Mark 5:29 NIV.)

Now we must be careful of what we ask for, even if it is asking for more faith, because God will allow a circumstance to occur for your faith to be tested! We look at those lives we consider more successful and idolize them, but we fail to see what they went through to get to where they are. The woman with the issue of blood had suffered for years. The Bible tells us she had gone to several doctors and spent a lot of money to only end up feeling worse. Imagine if the author Mark never provided those details before giving his readers the healing results. Today's society would have believed that she achieved it overnight without any sacrifice, faith, hope, endurance, or obedience to reach a point where she could finally heal. To hear about a healer that she has never known, fighting through a crowd of people while sick and weak, and having the confidence and gall to break the rules. This woman's faith was inspiring! During those days, it was unlawful for someone to touch another of his status and, on top of that, she was unclean because of her bleeding. She risked it all and came out on top! "Won't he, do it?" It is also important that whatever you ask of the Lord, be sure to throw in a request for preparation as well. The saying "when preparation meets opportunity" is true. There is nothing worse than asking for something, getting it, and then fumbling the ball. Know your; Why? Are you asking out of selfish ambition, or is your heart open to doing the will of God no matter what? We will not get it right all the time, but at least you got in the game and attempted a shot! So, keep going, keep fighting, and keep God first!

PERFORMANCE SAVIOR

In my therapy sessions, I repeatedly alluded to the fact that it had been torture trying to live up to the expectations I set for myself, along with the anxiety of having to perform in all aspects of my life. My entire existence has been performance-based. At work, at home in my role as a mother, as an athlete, in relationships whether romantic or platonic, etc. Think about it, at the end of every year, managers conduct an annual review for employees. Employers have all kinds of metrics and analytics on how you have helped their company succeed. As full-time mothers, God forbid you miss a few parent-teacher conferences, extracurricular activities or, better yet not breastfeed your child. You might face ridicule in the comment section of a perfect person's mommy blog! Think about the countless trades that happen in professional sports, due to how players perform or the amount of money one could generate based on not only their skills but on how they entertain.

Then there is the union of marriage. Now I am not married yet, but I know there are couples whose marital relationships are completely transactional. Each day is like swiping a credit card, hoping to receive reward points.

In writing this book, I wanted to be open and honest. In doing so, allow me to note that throughout my walk with Christ these past 7 years at certain times, it has been just that; performance-based and transactional. Let me explain. Feeling drained, I decided to turn to Christ as my own efforts were futile. Most of the time, I walked afraid of God. I feared that any wrongdoing would result in punishment and a definite arrival to the fiery furnace rather than the pearly gates. So instead of strolling like an heir, my feet timidly walked on eggshells, fearful of being a sinner and afraid of disappointing God. I did not want to be a hypocrite. The Bible tells us in,

(1 John 4: 16-18 NIV) "God is love. Whoever lives in love lives in God; and God in them. This is how love is made complete among us so that we will have confidence on the day of judgment: in this world we are like Jesus. There is no fear in love. But perfect love drives out fear because fear has to do with punishment. The one who fears is not made perfect in love."

This example shows me wanting to conduct myself flawlessly, trying to earn a love that he had already given. Instead of seeking God and who he is as my father, I was aiming for perfection. Though my reason for wanting to do things, his way laid the foundation along the road, it was fear that became the deciding factor for me to do well, instead of unconditional love. Throughout this expedition with Christ, this showed itself in several ways. As I continued to study his word, the fright of punishment diminished, but God noticing and commending my good works heightened. It came to the point where I wanted God to be immensely proud of me! Not realizing that my discipline is a far greater act than anything I could ever do for someone else. My problem was that I was not even considering God or asking his opinion before deciding to make a move. Again, as I continued in my word, prayer, and fasting, I quickly understood that anything we do for others, or any moves we try to make without God's consideration leads us to operate out of the flesh. The Bible tells us the flesh is self-seeking, and the heart is deceitful.

> *"The heart is deceitful above all things and beyond cure. Who can understand it?" (Jeremiah 17:9 NIV)*

There have been many other stages I went through as well in my walk with Christ. Allow me to tell you about another time that awakened my eyes to what he wanted to reveal to me about myself and his love for me. As mentioned before, God speaks to me through people and the things I hear, whether it be from a movie, sermon, TV show, etc. One day, while on social media, this woman made a video saying that believers are not inviting the Holy Spirit into their lives each day. She provided a mantra that she believed that we all should say every day. It said, and I quote.

> *"Good morning, Holy Spirit, I welcome you into my life. I welcome you into my day to lead and guide me with all truth beginning with the truth about me. Give me wisdom*

and knowledge make me love poured out. Let the words that I speak be filled with love so that anyone who meets me meets you and is arrested by your love." (Jimeki_j, Tik-Tok)

I said this consistently and remained regularly in my prayer closet. At this time, my son was gone for the summer with his dad and instead of trying to have a hot girl summer, it became a sanctified one. One day, while sitting in my prayer closet, my plea to God was for him to come sit with me. The request was not only for his presence, but for him to physically appear in my closet and sit with me! My question repeated itself so much so that after hoping and begging him to please come to take a seat with me, it brought me to a stream of tears. Instead of fulfilling my request to see him come down on his white cloud, he heightened my senses to notice him in people. The encounters I had with people thereafter felt heaven sent! One time, he used my good friend to show himself to me. Even though I had been imploring him to visit me in the flesh, another one of my requests was to have a glow about myself that was undeniable. My ask of him was this, "I have been through many seasons in this journey with you, but never a GLOW season. My exact words were, I want to glow! The type of glow that others can see all over me and they notice it without me saying anything. A, glow season! It could not have been more than a few days later when I attended a graduation party. A nice outdoor gathering in the backyard, enjoying family, food, and friends. I slipped out of the back gate and onto the sidewalk to take a hike up and down the street. After several strides back and forth along the pavement, I called my friend. Hey friend, I said, what are you doing? Some time went by as we continued chatting it up while on Face-time. Okay, let me stop with the term "Face-time." It is "Team Android" over here, so technically there was no Face-time, but you get the point. She says to me unexpectedly, "Friend, you are glowing, you look pretty." When I tell you the joy and laughter that erupted inside of me. To this day, she still does not know how those words that she said brought me even closer to God. You might be thinking, Yeah, but Mesha, friends tell each other that all the time. It's no big deal. My reply would be that understanding your friend and having a connection with your heavenly father is essential. Yes, my friend has often said those words to me "You look pretty" but for her to use the word "Glowing" specifically! You could not tell me it was not my God speaking to me! It blew my mind!

Of course, there are more of these stories. As mentioned before, there were other encounters with people and other things happening that let me know the good Lord was speaking to me. This is also where he exposed me as well. This situation helped me to understand my cry for him to sit with me, my savior complex behavior, my urge for freedom, and my fight to be the one to get my family out of financial ruin. Jesus continued to send me wonders of himself. Another time it happened, I stepped out of the shower wrapped in a cotton towel, as I was searching the dryer for underclothes, I casually said aloud, "God, I need some more underwear and bras." This was just me speaking outwardly to him as normal. A few days later, while speaking to my sister on the phone, she said, "Girl, I was shopping online at Victoria's Secret and ordered me some underwear and bras and I grabbed you some too!" After the laughter subsided, I informed her of my request a few days prior and she laughed with me as I confirmed to her that

God hears me. Now this is where the plot thickens. After her agreeing that God indeed hears us, my immature response was something like, "I hope he heard me about the bigger things I asked for." We continued to cackle, but it was not until sometime later God convicted me of my immature outburst. I am unsure what prompted this conversation with my Abba. I just remember feeling convicted about my statement. At that moment, he asked a simple but thought-provoking question. He said, *"Why are the things I do for you not enough?"* Now, both instances with my friend and sister blew my mind, but if I am being honest, it crossed my thoughts that these special moments that God displayed felt like a soft slap in the face. Let me explain. In my human mind, these moments proved what I already knew to be true, that God could hear me! So, if he could, why only give me pebbles and not the mapped-out *Habakkuk 2:2* list I had written?

"Write the vision, and make it plain upon tables, that he may run that readeth it." (Habakkuk 2:2 KJV).

Now, I will not front on God and act like a lot of the things that I had written failed to happen. They did, but it felt like the things that could afford me the life I believed was suitable for an heir were nowhere in sight. With every positive move forward, life came to beat me up and send me five steps back! Do you remember the classic game Mortal Kombat released in 1992? When the character Scorpion would tell his opponents, "Get over here" and then demolish them thereafter? That is how life grabbed your girl every time I was on a cusp, whether it be financial stability, discipline in a certain area of my life, or even just reaching a simple goal.

To reiterate, the plot thickened! When God asked me, *"Why are the things I do for you not enough?"* my immediate response was, *"Because I am not enough."* Whew! This response came to my mind so fast. This conversation with God, though simple and quick, summed up my whole 37 years of living on this earth. The reasons I performed all these years, the urge for me to be my family's savior, the toxic relationships endured, etc., all stemmed from this flawed character trait. I needed everything he did for me to be done grandly so that I could feel grand! I am convinced that he intentionally did these "small things;" knowing that I would get a kick out of it but also knowing the child he created. He knew the "small wins" would not suffice. He purposely did this to show me the truth about how I saw myself, and the truth is, I wanted the title of "Kingdom Heir" but did not understand or even think I was enough to achieve it. Through this walk with Christ, I have learned that there is nothing one can do to "achieve" this honor; it is already in our DNA!

"Now if we are children, then we are heirs—heirs of God and co-heirs with Christ, if indeed we share in his sufferings so that we may also share in his glory" (Romans 8:17 NIV).

JOURNAL

A MOMENT TO RELEASE

Have you ever asked God a question and had a response that was so undeniable that it was him? If so, let's unpack and process this situation. What was your first thought? Did you feel like you were tripping? What was your response to his answer? What was your Aha moment? Again, there is no pressure to write anything if you are not ready! You have the right to unpack and release at your own pace.

_____

_____
_____
_____
_____
_____
_____
_____
_____
_____
_____
_____
_____

A SAVIOR SENDS HELP

"For he will deliver the needy who cry out, the afflicted who have no one to help." (Psalms 72:12 NIV)

God has shown himself in my life throughout my journey with him. He has saved me from myself plenty of times and has sent benefactors who have altered my course of poor decisions, placing me on a better path. Like, for instance, my dad. I spoke about our daddy-daughter issues previously but allow me to show how he has helped me in his rearing. As mentioned before, your girl was not a fan of school and my grades showed it, especially in high school. If my memory serves me right, attending summer school was a requirement throughout high school because of my poor grades. If it was not for my dad insisting that I move in with him, I may not have graduated from high school. My dad provided me with a structure that I neglected to receive while living at home with my mother. Imagine being a young girl able to come and go as she pleases. It was a good thing that I had activities like sports to keep me busy or there could have been some risky things I could have been into. Now, between me and you, moving with my dad was not exciting for me. Just because I knew there would be order, curfew, rules, etc. What child in their adolescent mind would want to deal with that when they came from a dissimilar situation? It was as if I lived a double life. When at home with my mother, there were no actual rules, at least none she stuck to, and with my dad, it was rules, rules, and more rules! Now, as an adult, I am thankful for the structure my pops instilled in me. It was the discipline needed to help me deal with the hardships life would bring. Jesus is gracious that he will plant the right people in your life to steer you in the right direction. Have you ever met someone who influenced you to change, or they planted a seed of hope to keep you going another day?

Allow me to tell you about another amazing person who has helped shape the woman I have become today. Her name is Jennette Foster! Auntie Jennette is one of my dad's older sisters. In the summers, while staying with my pop's, I would often go to my aunt's house to hang out with her, my uncle, and my cousins while my dad worked. Auntie Jennette worked as an educator for decades with children, and in her later years before her retirement, she became a guidance counselor. Which suited her because of her caring nature, but make no mistake about it, Auntie was no push over and she ran a tight ship! She may have been a tough cookie, but boy did she love her some Mesha! She became a mother figure for me when I needed it the most. Growing up as a child, my upbringing did not involve going to church. The only real time I entered the church house was when I visited with my aunt in the summer. As a young girl going into church with her and witnessing those around me catch, what I now know to be the "Holy Ghost" initially had me shaken. I did not know what was going on or what was happening to these people. They would also speak in tongues, which had me convinced they were a little cuckoo for cocoa puffs, but, of course, as a child, it was new for me. The time spent in church with my aunt was cool, though, but seeing the members of the church do these things left me pondering. One day, while hanging at my aunt's house after going to church with her a few times, I asked her, "Auntie, do I have to know how to speak in tongues to go to heaven?" She chuckled and reassured me, "Honey, no, you do not have to know how to speak in tongues to become saved and go to heaven. All you must do is accept Christ as your Lord and Savior and believe and you will be saved."

"If you declare with your mouth, "Jesus is Lord," and believe in your heart that God raised him from the dead, you will be saved. For it is with your heart that you believe and are justified, and it is with your mouth that you confess and are saved. (Romans 10:9-10 NIV)

As an adult, I would like to thank my auntie for that type of reassurance, because children are very impressionable. If she had presented it negatively and condemned me for not being able to or told me, I would not go to heaven; who knows how that may have tainted my walk with Christ? Let me also take a moment to thank my father because, even though we did not attend church, he introduced me to Christ through Bible study. My dad would say, "Get to know him for yourself." That was another seed planted that later in my adult life reaped a harvest. It allowed me to remember that no matter what I've learned from someone in a pulpit or heard from listening to a podcast, I could always tap into the source by reading God's word and seeking him for myself.

Have you ever met someone who seemed not to be from this life? Someone you have met that helped you in some way and then it is like they vanished off the face of the earth. Or a stranger approached you, insisting that God told them to pray for you? This situation has happened to me. Let me explain. My son and I had to have been in Dallas, Texas, not even a year yet. During this time, I was not physically attending church, but I was tuning into services on YouTube featuring Pastors Michael and Natalie Todd of Transformation Church. Every year, the main pastors of the Church lead a 21-day Daniel fast. At this stage of my walk, I had not yet done a fast longer than 3 days. Not intentionally, anyway. So, with the challenge accepted, I committed to completing the 21-day Daniel's fast. Though the days seemed long, and the headaches lingered from lack of sugar, the fast started okay. For me, the last week was the hardest of all, because your girl needed sugar! Did you know that according to the American Heart Association, ***"American adults consume an average of 17 teaspoons of added sugar every day, over 2-3 times the recommended amount?"*** That last week had me like that plant in the 1986 film 'Little Shop of Horrors' talking about "Feed me!" Yes, your girl has a sweet tooth just like her dad. Not so much new candy that is out these days. I am old school when it comes to snacks. A good ole Charleston Chew, Little Debbie Zebra cakes, or my favorite chocolate pecan turtles! See, look at me going off on a sugar tangent! In the words of Mrs. Tabitha Brown, "Stay focused."

Anyhow, where was I? Oh yes, the stranger who came up to me and said God told her to pray for me. It may have been the spring of 2021. I picked my son up from football practice at his school. As I pulled into the parking lot and pulled into an open space, I got out of my car to watch the tail-end of practice. As practice ends and we are walking to the car; ahead of my son, this lady hops out of her car, comes up to me, and introduces herself. She says, this may sound weird, but God told me to get out and pray for you. Now, be mindful that my 21-day Daniel fast is over. I had made it through! During the fast, I remember feeling homesick and praying to God for abundance to happen in my life. Then, she asks me, "Do you mind if I hold your hand?" Now, I will not lie. My nerves kicked in. One, because this had never happened to me before, two, we were in the middle of a school parking lot and three, as the old folks would say, "Don't let everyone pray over you." As she placed her hands in mine, I could feel myself wanting to cry, but to tell you the truth, those tears did not fall until I got home and fell to my knees! The prayer she said itself is vague in my memory, but the words after I will not forget. She said, "God is with you, and he hears you. Don't give up." As we went our separate ways, my thoughts raced, but there was no doubt in my mind that God had her on an assignment that day! Now let's just take a moment and shout out the good sister for being obedient, because like the lyrics from the talented singer-songwriter Victory Boyd says*, "You never know if your light will be the hope for someone else that's all alone."* Savior, Savior, he sends helping hands!

Once I entered the car, my son asked, "mom what were you all doing," my response was, "praying!" You all, your girl cried like a baby when I got home. I made phone calls to any and everyone who would listen to my amazing encounter.

There have been several experiences in my life that led me to believe that God sent others to help me endure hardships and or remind me I was more than enough. The Bible tells us the power of life and death lies in the tongue, whether the verbiage we spew is positive or negative it matters! As a young child, being tall was a big insecurity for me. Enduring bullying at the time was not fun, and it played a key role in how I saw myself and my belief in how others viewed me. It was not until high school that embracing my unique height became the norm for me, and thereafter I stood tall and owned the height God blessed me with! Rocking my heels and all!

Another helper was this lady I came across; I still cannot recall her name or where she is to this day. It seemed like she came on a day that my spirit may have needed a pep talk. This encounter happened long ago, and I am uncertain at what time in my life it occurred, but years later, her words still echo in my head. Stepping out of my car, as I was walking into a gas station, she yells, "No, do not walk with your head down, hold your head up. You are beautiful, honey!" Still, to this day, I am not sure what made her say this to me. She could have felt the insecurity in me as I walked past, or, like I said before, it was just a friendly reminder. Now that I think about it, this might have taken place outside of the basketball world that I was previously immersed in. Let me explain. As mentioned before, accepting my height started in high school. In hindsight, it was so much easier or welcoming to love and embrace this unique stature, because during this time, most of my peers were tall, too. My high school team had four girls, including myself, who were over six feet tall, a few that were 5 '10-5' 11, and half of the boys' basketball team were tall as well. Being surrounded by people of loftiness continued into college, and for the first time, I felt normal and not like a freak of nature. Although, I would still get stares at the grocery stores while off campus grounds, but on campus it was normal for other student peers who may not have been tall to see athletes who towered over them. After graduating college, and then thrust into the life of "adulting," I think some part of me reverted to not feeling normal and not belonging again. This could be why God assigned her to me to deliver the message she gave! It was just what I needed to help boost my confidence in that moment, and to carry with me through this burdensome life.

THE COMPANY YOU KEEP

Remember when I spoke of all the different seasons I'd been through while on my walk with Christ? When the season of deciding who stays and who goes came along, it was an extremely uncomfortable stage for me. It was uncomfortable for two reasons. One because at the time confrontation was not something I did well. It bothered me to conflict with others, so much so that shutting down and cutting off all communication was the only choice. It was like "Cut you off" was my middle name. Later in life during therapy, I soon discovered the second reason. During that time, feeling exposed made me uneasy, particularly around certain individuals. Mostly those that I did not trust to be vulnerable around. At this stage, the good Lord had to rip the Band-Aid off until your girl was standing on an island all by herself. He was strategically isolating me. He was also teaching me how to have effective relationships with the new people I met, and to not have malice in my heart for the old relationships in which I left. Not everyone can go or should go with you in your new season. It came to a point where I could tell what was going to happen in a relationship or meeting someone new before it happened. Even at a new job or meeting a new individual, there would always be this sense that I was just passing through or they were just an assignment or a helping hand to get me to where God wanted me. This sense is still prevalent to this day. My antenna of discernment is up, and it is scary, to be honest with you. It's scary because it gives me the same insecure feeling all those years ago before high school and after my semi-pro days were over, of not fitting in anywhere. But, as stated before, of course he did not create me to fit in; with this stallion height, he handmade me to "Stand Out."

In this season of my life, the friendships of my brothers and sisters in Christ and who I would like to present myself as, are like the four friends of the paralytic man in the Bible. Have you all read that story in Mark chapter 2? So, BOOM right, Jesus had entered the town of Capernaum again, and the people of the town heard he had arrived. They came out to see him in droves, and there were so many people that there was no room at all for people to stand or sit to even see Jesus teach the good news! Four men tried to bring their friend, who was a paralytic, up to see Jesus so he could heal him. Now, I called the four men of the paralyzed man his friend, but scripture never said who they were or even their relation to him. After I continue telling you the story, you will understand why they had to have known him or been his friend. They stood on business, determined to get their friend the help he needed. Scripture says,

"Since they could not get him to Jesus because of the crowd, they made an opening in the roof above Jesus and, after digging through it, lowered the mat the paralyzed man was lying on," (Mark 2:4 NIV)

Now, do you see why I said they had to have loved this man and been his friend, brother, uncle, or something because they climbed onto the roof? They were determined to get him the help he needed from the one they believed to have healing hands. Do you have people around you who will stick with you during tough times? If you could not move, would they be willing to carry the weight for you? Better yet, are you that friend? We should practice being that for ourselves, as well as being what we want to see in the world.

The next person I would like to shine a light on is my sister. The same one who bought the undies for me! Yep, my big sister has been the most loyal person in my life. Granite, we have not always been as close as we are now, because of our age difference. She is six years older than me, so yes; I was the annoying little sister and let her tell it, the "snitch." Don't believe her guys; Mesha is no snitch! Okay, maybe I did a little, but hey that's what happens when you are the baby of the family. I am the youngest of three. My sister is the firstborn. At an early age, she had to assume adult responsibilities, and, like my auntie Jennette, she later became a mother figure for me. We started becoming closer, around my last year of college. This was a blessing because I did not have anyone, besides a close friend who also attended LSU. She was the only one at the time who could understand what I was going through at LSU. Although I don't think my sister could fully understand my plight, at least she was available for me to talk to and aid me monetarily. She was there when I was dirt poor. I remember being so hungry with nothing to eat that she ordered a pizza for me. At this time, I still lived in Louisiana, and she was in Missouri. There had been several times she had provided for me, whether it be buying me something to eat or helping on a bill. I will say that God knew I would need a helping hand and a sister's love to get me through the tough times. Thankfully, she is still in my corner today and I'm thankful for her every day!

There have been others in my life that I believe God had sent to aid me along this journey called life, and it is the one who came from my womb, my son! The day I found out I was pregnant; your girl had just come from basketball practice. After my basketball eligibility was up following the 2008 season, unfortunately, I could not enter the WNBA draft. So, to be close to the one thing that was dear to my heart, I continued playing by any means necessary. The Baton Rouge Heat was a semi-pro basketball team in Baton Rouge, Louisiana. When I say continued play by any means necessary, that is what I meant because I even took part in a YMCA league. On the way home from practice, I stopped and got an at-home pregnancy test. Before this, I had been feeling very sluggish. Getting down the court was like running with cement shoes on. I remember one day, while playing in a YMCA game, one guy who frequented the gym, who was a friend of both me and my son's father, said, "Your girl running slow, huh?" He made this statement while conversing with my son's father. After this, he had also mentioned to him that I had been playing slowly, and I might be pregnant. My son's father told me about this later and we laughed about it, not even realizing that he hit the nail right on the head!

Arriving at home after a long day of practice, I entered the bathroom to take a shower, but before stepping into the tub, I urinated on the pregnancy stick. Nervous as heck, I took my time washing up, praying that those results would come back negative. Frankly, we were not ready to be anyone's parents, nor were we financially ready to take on this responsibility. In fact, I had no actual plan for what life looked like after graduating. Then, I still had not come to grips with the one thing I loved the most that was slipping away. After pacing back and forth in the bathroom after getting out of the shower, procrastinating, to look at the stick for results, I mustered up the courage to do so. BOOM! Positive! Yes indeed, you are the mother! These results were problematic for me. You all do not understand this is not how my life was supposed to turn out! I am supposed to be on ESPN being announced as the number 1 draft pick overall, on my way to London to create my clothing line for tall women, opening a nonprofit, and thereafter getting married and having kids! I was in disbelief, shock, and denial, but God knew what I did not know. That my son Judah would help me in the fight to stay alive after the horrible breakup between me and basketball. God knew I would continue to go through the fire and would need something else to live for. The only thing is that God never intended for me to make my son my Savior. I did that of my own accord. In hindsight, I am sure God wanted me to run to him so that he could be the one I looked to for comfort, but instead, I clung to my son.

"Praised be to the God and Father of our Lord Jesus Christ, the Father of compassion and the God of all comfort, who comforts us in all our troubles, so that we can comfort those in any trouble with the comfort we ourselves have received from God." (2 Corinthians 1:3-4 NIV)

Don't get me wrong, bringing a child into this world should change you for the better, and help to make you more selfless, but in this life, there is only one who is our true anchor. It is a hard pill to swallow when you realize your children are not your own, but even they belong to God! Women are the portal that brings them into this world, but the gift comes from the creator!

There have been others in my life that I believe God had sent to be of help to me along the road. Like my cousin who has been a tremendous help since I moved to Dallas. Then there is Faith Church in Saint Louis, Missouri, where I became a member and was first baptized. Along with several others, I appreciated their encouraging words or them lending a helping hand up.

Now, I would like to share with you the greatest help your girl has ever received and how my Savior has guided me while on this long road of long-suffering! The Bible discusses long-suffering, but I naively assumed that once I was baptized and had accepted God as my Lord and Savior, life would resemble the often-used term on social media "A soft life." Boy was I not only wrong, but it showed that I was not reading my word at all. Can't we all tell when we are speaking to someone if they are believers or not? Or they have not read the Bible and have not had the Holy Spirit interpret the scriptures for them? That was me early on. (Still a work in progress) Honestly, I had not read my Bible regularly until about 3 years ago. My first time being immersed in water was at the age of 31 or 32 if I remember correctly. My dad had always told me that he refrained from getting me baptized as a baby because he wanted me to seek God for myself and to make that decision on my own. I am grateful he decided to do it that way, because pursuing God for myself allowed my heart posture to transform overtime. It reminded me of how God loves us and how he grants each one of us the opportunity to seek him because he has already chosen us. I committed to this endeavor 7 years ago and have been fighting to stay at God's feet ever since! Jesus aided me in perceiving myself as he perceives me and urged me to identify the root cause of why it took me so long to accept his love. When he asked me the question

"Why are the things I do for you not enough," my response was *"Because I am not enough."*

This conversation exposed my lack of confidence now that I could no longer perform. It forced me to look within, and it compelled me to pursue him, hoping he would save me from myself. Along this bumpy road, there was a part of me deep down that did not even think I was worth saving, because of all the things I had done that brought me such shame. Once we started building a father-daughter relationship, I didn't trust myself near his Holy presence. In my heart, I felt like, "Father you are too good for me," and he is, but as he did with the Samaritan woman, he met me right where I was, beat up, lost, bogged down in shame and pride searching for love in all the wrong places.

There is a full list of things that my father in heaven has aided me with, such as my anxiety. In

(Philippians 4:6-7 NIV) it says, "Be anxious for nothing, but in everything by prayer and supplication, with thanksgiving, let your request be made known to God and the peace of God, which transcends all understanding, will guard your hearts and your minds in Christ Jesus."

Some of the anxiety felt was solely because of my bad choices. Does anyone else love horror films? I know I did! Not only did your girl watch horror films, but I also indulged in real-life killing-death shows and movies, such as Dr. G the Medical Examiner, Untold Stories of the ER, or the movie The Craft. These shows and movies had me up at all hours of the night, watching with the lights on. Crazy right? The fear of death consumed me, leading to a morbid curiosity and obsession with watching such things. We, as believers, must be careful of the things we watch and listen to because they can seep into our hearts and minds. Instead of fixating on God, we can become obsessed with the very thing that is keeping us bound. It took me years to give up watching these types of things, but once I did, the nightmares stopped. Have you ever had a dream where you were falling and right before hitting the ground, you woke up? Or a dream where someone was trying to murder you, and you could not move or even wake up because of sleep paralysis? These are the things that would happen to me due to my mind being preoccupied with death and watching these types of shows. I appreciate the support from God that saw me through these matters.

My life traumas have also aided my anxiousness. Take, for instance, the several car accidents I have been in. Allow me to tell you another story. This was back in Louisiana. I was about 8 months pregnant, had no money, and had just scraped up enough change to at least grab me a nice cold slushy from 7-Eleven. During this time, your girl, although with-child, could not eat or get the proper nutrients needed to have a healthy baby. My lack made me fearful that my son would come into this world malnourished. Your girl was eating once a day if that. So, you could understand how exciting it was for me to get this big gulp I had been craving! While driving back home from the store, approaching the intersection, BOOM, another driver, turns in front of me and strikes the left side of my car. There sits my slushy drink on my lap instead of in my stomach. I was beyond pissed! Honestly, not because of the accident, and I know you are like "Wait, what Mesha? What about the unborn child growing inside of you, or what about your life? Do you know how long it took me to scrape up enough change to pay for that slushy? My son and I needed that cold slush! I am positive that this was not even the accident that triggered my anxiety. I just wanted to share this story because I thought it was comical how upset I was over not finishing my drink. Now understand when you have so much trauma or when life is just doing its thing, this incident was just another day in the life of an ex-superstar player, who was now seeing life from another perspective. Even though this view of poverty was familiar, during this time it was a thousand times worse, because I had this unborn child growing inside of me, with no real plan on how we were going to take care of him.

The accident that left me shaken and filled with worry was the one that happened in my hometown of Saint Louis, Missouri. Again, my sidekick; my son and I were riding on the highway, him in the backseat strapped in his booster, making our way to our destination in the rain. A driver who hydroplaned as he was coming onto the highway struck us. He was speeding as he slid across one lane, knocking us from the middle lane to the far-left lane, causing us to hit and break the median. Thank God we're not too cool for the safe belt. Thank God that he allowed both of us to walk away from that accident with nothing but a slight gash in the neck of my son from the seat belt, catching him and a slightly bruised knee from me hitting the steering wheel. Unfortunately, after this mishap, I still had work, my son had school, appointments, etc. and the thought of driving again was terrifying! One day while driving the rental car I received after the accident, my mind played tricks on me. If you stopped and started singing the song, you are my type of person! Anyhow, the roads began to close, and the more I drove, the narrower they became. This left me feeling weak, as though I was about to pass out, which led me to panic. This is where the good Lord came through for me. Not only did he bring us out alive, but it was possibly the first time I realized that my mind was a powerful tool and that controlling it was something I could do with just speaking.

**"And God said, "Let there be light," and there was light"
(Genesis 1:3 NIV)**

As I am driving, I repeatedly say, "Mesha, you are okay. This is not real. You are safe." It was so weird because the moment I stopped, the fear started creeping back up and the roads started closing again, so I had to say it repeatedly. Another way God assisted me in the situation was by giving me the gift of having a profound sense of humor. Being able to find the humor in anything is a wonderful gift to possess. As I was riding in the same rental car with my sister one day, I could feel a panic attack boiling up. I said out loud to my sister in the most non-serious way possible, "Girl, these roads are closing in on me." I vaguely remember the jokes that came after, but I recall the laughs we had and then the actual concern my sister had as she said, "Girl, do you need me to drive." That attack did not get the best of me, and we arrived safely at our destination.

I am overwhelmed with gratitude for the unwavering guidance and support of the Holy Spirit throughout my life. God aided me when he used basketball as an outlet for me. My home situation before moving with my father was not a great environment for a child to grow up in. God blessed me with an outlet that I loved and allowed me to travel and experience things my siblings did not. God also helped me get over my fear of death. Not that I would not be terrified if I faced death. It's just to say that it is not a continuous scary movie always playing in my mind or me creating scenarios in my head repeatedly. Death frequented my thoughts around the clock. All day every day for years and by the grace and the love of God, he has removed those cumbersome thoughts. Sometimes, those images try to creep up, and when it rarely happens, I rebuke them right away in the name of Jesus! Can I get an amen? Nowadays, I focus on avoiding spiritual emptiness rather than physical death. So, I am thankful to God for teaching me how to fight now! Facing the devil's malevolent plans can be challenging, but let's face it, it's not always the devil;

sometimes it's battling against our own sinful desires. Battling against my wants often created barriers between me and God.

Of course, there are so many other stories that I can say about how God has been a fighting force in my life. From providing shelter and protection for me in my homelessness, allowing me to walk out of every car accident that I have been in, injury-free, to not condemning me for my past transgressions. As we continue to blossom as friends, my prayer is not only that he continues to be my refuge and my comforter, but that I can inherit his unwavering love, affection, and correction.

"I no longer call you servants because a servant does not know his master's business. Instead, I have called you friends, for everything that I learned from my Father I have made known to you." "You did not choose me, but I chose you and appointed you to go and bear fruit—fruit that will last. Then the Father will give you whatever you ask in my name." (John 15: 15-16.)

Savior, Savior, he sends helping hands!

JOURNAL

_____

A MOMENT TO RELEASE

Do you have anyone in your life like my aunt, sister, or even a stranger who planted a seed of hope or gave sound advice? Maybe you have someone, or perhaps a moment you experienced with someone, that started your introduction to who God is. If so, release it and give them thanks for the spark they gifted you with. If not, feel free to express your meeting with the Savior and how it has changed your life.

_____

_____

_____

_____

_____

_____

_____

_____

_____

_____

_____

CHAPTER

5

BLESS IT SAVIOR

"Put it in my hands I'll give it back to you you'll see lord." Mali Music

Have you ever received a sweet no-look pass from Jesus and fumbled the ball? I have plenty of time while on this journey with him. Take, for instance, the time God gave me specific instructions to sell my car! Let me explain. God had been gracious enough to allow me to pay off my car in a lump sum. Leading up to me paying it off. I had made a conscious decision to be a good steward over the money that came in. During this time, I was blessed with a job that allowed me to earn an okay amount of money, more than I had ever made before. From my employment, there were monthly bonuses on top of a salary; things were going well for me, especially seeing that I had just come out of a dry place financially. I was heavy in my word, tithing everything that God allowed to come my way. So, it was only right to be a good steward of my finances and to get out of debt. Creating a plan on how to pay off all my debt was easy, but doing it was the hard part. After looking over financial videos on YouTube, I used Dave Ramsey's "7 Baby Steps" to get out of financial ruin. Of course, reading the Bible about stewarding and finances helped along this journey as well. Savior, Savior Bless it, Savior!

Not only was there job income to help with paying my debt, but there was income from the sale of my home as well as the income from an unfortunate incident, which led to me retaining a lawyer. I know you are itching to know what my unfortunate incident was, right? Okay, since you asked! Your girl was bitten by Cujo! Have you seen that movie? An old classic. Picture it, right? You are just minding your good ole business being an "essential worker" trying to get the people their packages, and boom you are jumped by not one but two dogs! Okay, you can stop laughing now! No, it is cool, laugh, I do! I often joke about this incident with friends and family. Look at God, helping me to find the laughter in tragedy and making a way for me to carry out my goal of paying off my debt. One could think, well Mesha, this situation is not funny. Granite, it was not humorous at the time, but even days after I was able to find the funny in the situation. My growth and walk with Christ have taught me that everything, and I mean everything that happens in our lives, can work out for the good of those who love the Lord. I want to tread lightly when saying everything because I have not been through every tragedy that one could face, but for those calamities I have faced, God instilled in me the gift of humor to help me through. To some, my sense of humor may be a little weird. I am the person laughing at those TikTok videos of disabled people or comedians who make fun of themselves during traumatic times in their lives. I enjoy the fact that they are not taking themselves so seriously that they cannot laugh or have joy in hard circumstances. Laughter uplifts and nourishes the soul.

Okay, now back to the main point of this story. In conclusion, your girl paid off the known debt, which included all the things on my credit report as well as some things that didn't make it to my credit report. All except for my twelve-thousand-dollar student loan. Yes, in the earlier chapter, there had been mention of me receiving full ride scholarships from both colleges I attended, which is a fact. This loan came from me having the bright idea of going back to school to receive a double bachelor's degree in what I originally wanted to pursue all along. That is another story for another day and possibly another book or a cinema project!

In Dave Ramsey's 7 Baby Steps, he says to pay off everything but your home, and since I was selling my home, the next biggest debt was my student loan. After paying my car off, I felt accomplished but also a little sick from having to pay that much in a lump sum. As I have learned throughout this walk with God, there are levels to your faith. Like the seven baby steps for your finances, you start with the smallest debt first, then work your way to the largest. It seems like it is the same steps we take in our faith in Jesus.

"I tell you the truth, if you have faith as small as a mustard seed, you can say to this mountain, move from here to there and it will move. Nothing will be impossible for you." (Matthew 17:20 NIV)

The seed planted was intended for me to become a good steward, and God would handle the rest to bring forth the harvest. Now you are thinking, yes well, you were only stewarding because you were already in your place of abundance. Allow me to use basketball analogy. You were not in the gym with me shooting. One of the greatest gospel duos "Mary; Mary" said in their song called *"God in Me."*

> ***"But what they don't know is when you go home and get behind closed doors, man, you hit the floor, and what they can't see is you're on your knees."***

We do not know everything that it took for someone to gain the success that you see now. Nonetheless, I planted the seed, and God created the harvest, but to reach the next level of my faith, a test was presented before me. As quickly as I received it, it was being taken away. My car had been paid off for only about 11 months when I was laid off from my job. Here I am debt-free, with no income. Part of **Dave Ramsey's "7 Baby Steps"** is to have an emergency fund of one thousand dollars and then save 3 to 6 months of expenses. After aggressively paying off major items, I was able to save the emergency fund and 1 month of expenses. While trying to keep a positive attitude, I brushed off, being unemployed and hoped that another job would come soon. A couple of months had passed and out of the excessive amounts of applications filled out, I was still jobless. This is where my faith would undergo another test, and I was convinced that God was instructing me to sell my car. Wait! What God? He could not be ordering me to sell this car, not the one he graciously allowed me to pay off! Those were my thoughts. "Wait! What?" Not my beloved Shay Baby!

Yes, that was her name. I loved that car! In hindsight, it is also my belief that through this test, God wanted to see two things from me. One, would I trust him and two would I obey him? In my Norbit voice, don't you just love tests? So, a long story short, yep, I failed, but what my Father in heaven wanted prevailed, anyway. The last thing I could do was save Shay Baby from being sold to someone else. Savior, Savior, bless it, Savior!

Instead of putting the car up for sale as I was instructed, your girl had the bright idea of getting a title loan. I basically told God, "No, I think there is a better way we both can get what we want." It reminded me of the story of Sodom and Gomorrah. When the angels gave specific instructions for Lot to flee to the mountains. Lot pleaded with them to allow him to go to a small nearby town. Lot seemed to doubt that he and his family would find security far from the impending destruction God was about to bring upon the city. In particular, the same with me. I could not fathom being without a car, or later having to finance another vehicle, so I came up with my plan and desire for a life I didn't even create. Here I am, not able to change the color of my very own head without using chemicals, not clairvoyant, and with no ability to even resurrect myself, if necessary, and yet dare to create this alternative plan.

After Lot begged the angels, they granted his request and informed him they would not overthrow the town of Zoar, which he wanted to flee. So, boom! Once Lot arrived in Zoar, scripture says, "the Lord rained down burning sulfur on Sodom and Gomorrah" (Genesis 19:24) and the town where Lot was, happened to be so close that he could see the burned vegetation and smoke. So, because Lot was afraid of what he saw, guess where he ended up! Yes, you guessed it, he ended up in the mountains where he had been instructed to go initially.

Do you all know that it was the same outcome pertaining to my situation? After getting the title loan on Shay Baby, the payments for the loan became so much that those unemployment checks would not suffice. The Lord knew I would not find a job as soon as I had hoped. He knew the plans he had for me. I ended up having to sell the car anyway to get from under the enormous loan debt. Now, I try not to get in the habit of playing the game of should of, could of, would of. In this walk, I have learned to keep the past in the past, learn from the lessons, and try not to repeat the same mistakes. If you take nothing else from this book, remember this gem in the Bible: *"obedience is better than sacrifice." (1 Samuel 15:22 NIV)*

During this time, I found myself in the wilderness. Although I had experienced plenty of rough times in my life, this time felt different. It felt painful and different from before. Unlike the times before I was saved, this time I knew I was in the presence of God and at least trying to live a Christ-led life. Honestly, that made the growing pains worse, because again, it made me feel like I was doing everything wrong and that my efforts were not good enough. Now, yes, I did not obey what God said when he told me to sell my car, but my thoughts were "God I am genuinely trying, there is no need to crush me this much." During this time, there was nothing I could do but sit in it with God. Not even privy to the fact that I was in this wilderness season. This never crossed my mind until going to a service on one Sunday. Dr. Conway, lead pastor of One Community Church, preached a sermon called "Overcoming Spiritual Dryness." He preached from the book of *Ezekiel, chapter 37.* In this chapter, the children of Israel had lost all hope. It says in the Bible,

"Then he said to me: Son of man, these bones are the people of Israel. They say our bones are dried up and hope is gone; we are cut off." (Ezekiel 37:11 NIV)

Even though they were connected to him, they still had no life in them. Look at chapter 37 verse 8 "I looked, and tendons and flesh appeared on them and skin covered them, but there was no breath in them." This could have been the same with me. Despite years of praising, reading the word, praying, and fasting, during this season, I stayed connected to my father but lacked spiritual growth because of my disobedience. Unlike the people of Israel, I had faith to speak enough to my financial situation, but to get to that next level, my obedience should have done the talking for me. Your girl was back in a financially dry place like I had been for most of my life. You can imagine me being so confused and disappointed. Here I am, taking the initiative to be a good steward and yet ended up falling flat on my face, monetarily and spiritually. This was not the prosperity gospel pastors preached about. Remember when I mentioned before about not mentioning the should of, could of, would of? I wondered what would have happened if I had just obeyed God that day and sold my car! Maybe nothing would have happened, or just maybe my obedience to God that day would have positively influenced my faith walk with him.

Now that I had been walking with God, in the moments of what felt like defeat, I could actively search for the lessons that could be learned from these unfortunate ordeals. In this situation, there were several lessons taught, such as when you hear God tell you to do something; move expeditiously. The second lesson was the confidence that I needed to know that I had the ability to steward my finances well. This let me know that if God blessed me with more, I would know what to do and how to handle it. Also, if he ever asked for it back, I would leave my hand open instead of clinching on to what was never mine to begin with. The third lesson I learned from this situation was that even though I was bogged down in debt, I could focus on developing character traits like self-discipline and generosity from the fruit of the spirit, which helped me in getting out of debt. Finally, another important lesson I learned was creating a plan and executing that plan but also being able to embrace life when having to pivot or deviate from said plan.

Throughout this book, I have provided plenty of stories of my rebellious nature outside of being delivered, and some after being saved. The Lord enlightened me on how my rebellious behavior had trickled over into my relationship with him. In the past year, I understood how my need to go against authority has hindered me from growing in all aspects of my life. As said, mostly everyone in power in my life had misused their authority in some way. Even those who may not have been in an authoritative position, but whom I trusted. From close family to basketball coaches, managers, boyfriends, and former co-workers, which made it hard for me to trust people. Especially after being used and abused by those who said they loved me or called themselves my friend. Now, I am not perfect, but if I do care for you, I will go the extra mile to help you and uplift you. So, when things or people hurt me, they affect me! Nowadays, I am learning to lean into the pain and be okay with crying. I am also learning to endure discomfort, as well as prioritizing guarding my heart. One night, while lying in bed with the lights off, I reflected on what God had been showing me about my defiant spirit. There I was brainstorming, trying to sort through this character flaw, when I thought to myself. "To get rid of all this defiance, God, just give me something I am great at, like I was with basketball." I said to God, "Now I know to keep my hand open instead of holding on to it and making it an idol." At that same moment, another thought came, asking, "Did you love basketball as much as you think you did?" "Or did it start as love and end in lust because it became a safe outlet and wonderful haven for you to perch under?" Moments later, other ideas of conversation made their way into my line of thought. If my dedication to basketball stemmed solely from duress, safety, or comfort, had I ever committed to anything willingly? Soon after that notion came, another one arose that said, "Well, we know you didn't come to God willingly. I mean you said it yourself that you were sick and tired of being sick and tired of doing things your way." "So, if you didn't choose God willingly and nor did you choose basketball readily, have you ever given yourself to anything or anyone?" That night I wept like a newborn baby fresh out of its mother's womb! I could not believe that I had spent my entire life like this! Existing instead of being, wishing instead of doing, watching instead of participating, and not wanting to know the one who created me for love, but for selfishness. Throughout this journey with Christ, I had shed so many tears, but that night, the weeping hit my soul. When God says in scripture **"You didn't choose me, I chose you," (John 15:16 NIV).** Is true! The second definition of the word "choose," according to Oxford Languages, is "deciding on a course of action, after rejecting alternatives." We all come into this world with no desire to automatically "Choose" the Lord, but after life rejections, we seek understanding to make sense of the world and in our trouble, therefore choose him after the fact. Some look for it in sage, crystals, and astrology, and some, like me, have looked for it in their children, relationships, and or identifying themselves through sports. When you feel yourself searching for clarity of the world and your circumstances, before you look at things that have no validity, remember what Jesus says in (*John 15:5 NIV*).

"I am the vine; you are the branches. If a man remains in me and I in him, he will bear much fruit; apart from me, you can do nothing."

Allow me to tell you another story about how your girl fumbled the ball. So, as you know, I have been an athlete my entire life. The second I recognized that my basketball career was over, and I attended a 9 to 5 regularly is the day I also stopped working out. A part of me deep down hated working out in the first place but only did it so that I could play the game I loved. Understand that God will always send you warning signs before something happens because he sent the message through my dad who told me not to stop working out and being active. This conversation happened years before the incident. Let me explain. For about a good decade, after not playing and working a 9 to 5, I had not worked out, if not most times at all. On this day, my body had enough of not being cared for. It happened the moment I went to sit back on the couch after getting up to do something. As soon as my bottom hit the seat cushion, a shock of nerve pain went through my whole body, which left me not able to walk for a few days. I don't mean limping here and there; I mean having to army crawl just to get to the restroom. Besides birth pains, there had been no physical pain I had experienced that had been to that extent. Honestly, I would have rather had another child without an epidural, than feel sciatic nerve pain like this! When I look over the story of my life thus far, the constant disobedience I have displayed has been unacceptable, and to think I have been claiming to be a follower of Christ. Thank you to God for blessing me with a cousin who is a doctor. They both helped me walk again. Quiet as kept once I could walk, your girl exercised every day right up until I didn't! Go ahead, judge me because I judged me. We often take things for granted. We take God for granted. Because of his merciful nature and gracefulness, we feel entitled to disrespect him. It is disheartening and discourteous if you think about it. The saying is, *"Procrastination is the assumption that you have more time." Unknown*. We all have an expiration date, but none of us knows when or what time it will happen. So, learn from me, when God sends you a sign and puts the gift of life in your hands, don't dishonor him by squandering the days you have left. I am still learning how to be better, a better person and a better daughter to him. It is hard, but it's an everyday decision.

If you have noticed this entire book thus far, I have spoken about my insubordinate conduct. Often, we can focus on the things we have not done but never give ourselves some grace and acknowledgment of the things we have done consistently or correctly. I need to be better at recognizing this, even if it is something we may consider small. My journey of eating healthier started with me cutting back on drinking soda, and about 10 years later, I can say that out of 365 days of the year, my soda intake is seldom! That is an accomplishment for someone like Kel who loved not orange soda, but Pepsi. From there I was able to cut out pork and then beef from my diet. The momentous change came when discovering that chicken was the real enemy. Allow me to give you a little backstory. Growing up as a young girl, my menstrual cycles were extremely painful, to where I would have to miss school one or two days every month. If I had to put my physical pain in order, it would be the sciatic pain first, then the childbirth, and then my menstrual cramps. I could keep no food down and I would throw up the lining of my stomach. Although the birth of my son helped with my cramps, it was cutting back on eating chicken that stopped me from having severe cramping, if any at all. I have done so much research over the years trying to find a solution to my problem. Finding out that it was chicken, and dairy as well, blew my mind. I believe that nowadays the chicken we consume are injected with so many hormones, which can lead to hormonal imbalances during an already temperamental time.

The other areas of my life where I want to acknowledge that I have been consistent include reading the word and pursuing the Lord. Out of my seeking came a wonderful awareness of the areas of my heart that needed worked on, and understanding how much Jesus loves me despite of my flaws. Our relationship has grown so much over the years. God has shown through his word the magnitude of his sacrifice for the world and has set a notable example for us all on how to be dedicated to our father's business!

I remember having a discussion with God in my kitchen as I was washing the dishes. Aloud, my question to him was "Why do all my blessings come in spurts?" Again, he says very quickly, "*Because you are consistent in spurts.*" At that very moment, while rinsing off the dishes, complete laughter comes from my mouth as I shake my head in agreement. Being consistent has been one of the hardest things for me to do. It is as if, over some time, routines become too repetitive, and the task becomes boring. In one of my therapy sessions, I spoke about this. There were problems with me being able to see things through to the end, and as our sessions continued, we recognized that perhaps others and my expectations could have been the root of the problem. Routines force me to be disciplined, which won't allow me to rebel and do what I want to do at the moment. My thought is that the root of the problem, besides the fact that I believe I may have ADHD, stems from the hurt that basketball caused. Let me explain. Picture placing all your eggs in one basket. Basketball was the only thing I had ever given over two committed decades to. It seemed like I had trained myself unconsciously to avoid situations where I could put all my effort into something but not reap the rewards. It is super weird and something through which I am still working. I remember explaining to my therapist that no matter how things are going, whether well or badly, it will end abruptly. Granite sometimes there have been life circumstances that hindered me from completing a project, tasks, or executing a business plan. Take, for instance, my lack of finances, but in all honesty, deep down, no matter the good or bad circumstances, my efforts would have come to a halt. Although I am still a work in progress with being consistent and obedient, as a reminder, I revert to the story of Noah building the ark. What if Noah didn't listen to God? Or better yet, what if he listened only partially and neglected to follow God's detailed instructions on building the ark? If you have read the story of Noah's Ark, then you understand God was very particular in his directions to Noah.

"This is how you are to build it: The ark is to be 450 feet long, 75 feet wide, and 45 feet high. Make a roof for it and finish the ark to within 18 inches of the top. Put a door in the side of the ark and make lower, middle, and upper decks." (Genesis 6:15-16 NIV)

God laid out every instruction. No matter how much time it took, nor the push-back from naysayers who thought he was insane, Noah remained submissive to what God instructed him to do. These days I am growing and learning how to accept the responsibilities of life while appreciating the times of pain just as much as I have ravished the good. I am also learning to be okay with shining, so much so that I leave a positive mark on the world for generations to come. There is so much that we as humans have inside of us, it would be a shame to not give it to the world. Miles Monroe once said, *"If your vision dies with you, then you have failed."* So, God, I pray that as long as I have breath in my body, may I continue to share the good news, be of service to those around me, and leave the fruit of my vision for those who come after me. Allow me to steward what you lay in my hands while continuing to inspire, illuminate, and ignite each person I encounter to be a light. Savior, Savior, Bless it, Savior! Amen.

JOURNAL

A MOMENT TO RELEASE

Has God ever set you up for an alley-oop and you missed terribly? Has he ever placed the things you asked for right in the palm of your hand and you realized you were not ready for it? Better yet, has God ever given you a specific direction and instead of obeying him, you did what you thought was best? If any of these things have happened to you, feel free to write about it below.

_____

_____

_____

_____

_____

_____

_____

_____

_____

_____

_____

_____

FROM TRYING TO SAVE, TO DOING MY PART

"You are the light of the world. A city on a hill cannot be hidden. Neither do people light a lamp and put it under a bowl. Instead, they put it on its stand, and it gives light to everyone in the house." (Matthew 5:14-15 NIV)

I believe my goal all along was to be effective in this world! To understand that I could complete the assignment agreed upon between me and God, before he even formed me in my mother's womb. We are all searching for substance, for something that we know to be true and real in this life. Some spend their entire lives seeking but never finding it. I remember speaking to a friend one day, telling her I had not found that thing, that thing that provided me with the same comforts, security, and confidence that basketball afforded me. Now, while on my 7-year journey, I understand I would never find it in relationships with men, in sports, in my child, in stuff that gives instant gratification, but only in the one who created me. This life is not our own and we are here on assignment, not here for personal gain, but to be a light! Can you imagine a world where no one had to worry about themselves because they trusted their neighbor had their back? A planet where everyone was of service to each other, and not seeking the glory for themselves, but always giving the glory to God?

Often, I wondered what my purpose on this earth was, and then I realized we are all here to be of service to each other, do our part in this world, glorify the Lord, and spread the good news. Once I figured that out, the next question was in what capacity should I be of service? This took me down a rabbit hole after my basketball career was over because it was my opinion that athleticism was all I had, and the only gift God gave me. Having spent years trying and failing at different things left me questioning my worth and sense of being! Take, for instance, the plethora of jobs I've had over the years from washing cars, bussing tables to mortgage, you name it and I'm quite sure I have done it! When I was young, my father never wanted me to get a job. He was adamant about me getting a scholarship so that it would pay for my education. He would also say, "Mesha, you need to focus on school and basketball. Don't worry about getting a job." At that time, I should have listened, but in hindsight, not having any work experience hindered me after college if I am honest.

My very first job was the shortest employment in employment history! We could have been in the Guinness Book of World Records. When I say we, I mean me and my best friend around that time. Let's just call her Mickey and I will be Denise aka NiSi! Again, if you know, you know! To get hired, you either needed to know someone or have some type of experience, and we had none. First-year students or sophomores in high school with no prior working experience and no one to hook us up, but we did not let that stop us. Although I am not sure how this came about us working for an ice cream shop, it happened. If I remember correctly, we frequented this place and asked the manager working there if they were hiring. To our surprise, he said yes! Brace yourself, this story goes left quickly! Do you remember the hilarious stand-up bit by one of the original Queens of Comedy? Sommore? When she said, "That men should come with side effect warnings like the commercials have for medications?" She was right! As soon as we asked him if the company was hiring and he opened his mouth to say yes, BOOM, he should have immediately lit up with a neon box beside his head that read "Side effects: shady, liar, thief, and jail time soon approaching."

Okay, allow me to get to the meat of this story. Not sure how the rest of the conversation went, but Mickey and I started working that same day. This should have been the first warning sign. The second sign came 20 minutes later when he left us unattended while he made a midday bank run. No proper training, no written paperwork, and two naive young girls still wet behind our ears, who were slowly figuring out how to operate the cash register. Forty-five minutes had passed and our manager, let's just call him Antonio, was nowhere to be found! We were running out of everything: waffle cones, napkins, chocolate ice cream and we did not know what to do or who to call, seeing that Antonio never left us his contact information. Sweating, panicked, and in complete shambles after turning away several customers due to not having anything. The horror continued as it was approaching closing time, and he still had not returned. We had made little money that day, and not to mention, Antonio had taken most of the funds to make a "bank run." Thankfully, a person who had been working there came into the store. I do not recall the details of the conversation with the lady, but to make a long story short, we had been hoodwinked and bamboozled! Antonio had stolen the money and left us to take the fall! Although the hilarious TV show "Everybody Hates Chris" that aired in 2005 and was based on the life of the famous comedian Chris Rock had not yet aired. Mickey and I both felt just like Chris did after every episode ended, when it said, "Everybody hates Chris!"

To this day, I am still wondering and asking God what does it look like to be purpose-filled? Or should we even be worried about being "In Purpose?" Honestly, I still don't think I have stepped into what God has for me, but I know I am trying and am in position to receive what he has for me when the time comes. I also believe that instead of spending most of our time pondering over our purpose on this earth, we could better use that time to position ourselves to hear from God and obediently follow his instructions.

Allow me to share this story of how my father in heaven dropped a word in my spirit that helped me understand how he works and how faith works. When I first moved to Dallas in 2020, your girl had to give it another shot at getting my teeth straightened. My first attempt with Smile Direct Club's aligners did not yield positive results for me. One reason is that I did not have enough discipline to keep up with the trays, and another reason is that they straightened my teeth in half the time, which hurt badly! While sitting in my orthodontist's chair the day before I got my braces off, the doctor informed me, "Mesha, your midline's are slightly off just a tad, but the great thing is that your canines are positioned in the right place. Therefore, we will not worry about your midline's, and you can get your braces off tomorrow!" I was so happy to hear the good news. The next day, as I was brushing the gates on my teeth, getting ready to head back up to the orthodontist's office to get them removed, the Lord dropped a word in my spirit. He said, "***You may not always feel aligned with me, but you are positioned in the right place.***" This is for every one of you, like me, who does not know in what capacity your purpose should look like, or maybe you are having a tough time hearing the voice of God in the wilderness season. I am here to give you the same word the good Lord gave me! If you stay at his feet, pray, be persistent in pursuing him through reading the Bible, repent, and be obedient, you may not always feel aligned with him, but you would be positioned in the right place! Prepared to inherit whatever he has for you!

BE THE LIGHT

"Your word is a lamp to my feet and a light on my path,"
(Psalms 119:105 NIV)

Be the light you want to see in the world. For a long time and sometimes even now, being a light is frightening. Not as much as being it for others, because I am great at recognizing it in everyone else. Even though at certain times, I used my gift of encouragement to feed my soul, I wholeheartedly believe that is a part of who God has made me to be, an encourager. For most people, being at the forefront is what they strive to do, but for me, the only time I felt invincible was while dominating on the court. Foolishly, I recall saying that the basketball court was my sanctuary because it gave me my set of superpowers! Now, as a 37-year-old woman, I accept what **Psalms 46:1 says, "God is our refuge and strength, an ever-present help in trouble."**

Another one of my top basketball movies, was the iconic film "Coach Carter. (2005)" If you have not seen this movie, you should! It is in my top 5 best basketball movies of all time. Life has had us all face the same question Coach Carter, played by yet another supreme movie star Samuel L. Jackson, when he asked, "What is your deepest fear?" Can you answer that question? Have you sat and thought in depth about this hefty question? If you have responded to this query and your answer is uncertain or it involves vanity or some phobia, you may have missed the point. Not to say those things are not valid, but let's go deeper, shall we? "What is your deepest fear? Throughout the film, Coach Carter repeatedly asked this to one of the most troubled players on the Richmond High basketball team. There was a bewildered look on the young man's face every time he asked this query. Have you ever struggled to answer this question? I have crossed-examined myself throughout my life with this question and considered the answer to be failure. As maturity set in, I understood that failure did not intimidate me as much as I thought. It has always been a part of me to try, stop, start, and fail, whether it be a new hairstyle, clothing choice, or trying to start a business. There have been plenty of risks taken in my lifetime. It was my light that frightened me the most! In my fear of shining there gave credence to defeat. Deep down inside, I knew if I were to submit to who lives within me; Jesus Christ, I would be vulnerable for the world to crucify.

"It is not our darkness, but the light that most frightens us." -Marianne Willamson

I would be accessible to the world's expectations and even the presumptions of myself. After fighting for so long, the responsibility of being a LIGHT, I hope that from here forward I courageously step into the spotlight! Not for my sake, but for the one who sacrificed his life for me and for those who have my obedience tied to their destiny. The one who gave me the gift of athleticism, writing, creating, and the desire to inspire others, and most importantly, he who has taught me how to see myself as he sees me. May my efforts in co-writing this book with the Lord, be like the character Leroy from the classic 1985 movie "The Last Dragon," afford me the opportunity to find the GLOW within!

Writing this book is a part of me doing the work that is needed in the world. Sharing my testimony and spreading the good news of Jesus in this way will hopefully inspire, illuminate, and ignite the person reading this to be a light that the world needs to see. I often used to ask God, "How can the life I live aid someone else, when it seems like I have nothing going for myself?" Throughout this journey, God has provided me with understanding this question. Even though my growth has been in obscurity, it does not mean that those around me are not and cannot be affected by it. One gift God gave me was unlocked during my time of anonymity, and it was writing. Before I started drafting this book, I created a blog called "My Height; My Crown." There was an article that I wrote called "Four reasons obscurity can be great." The four reasons provided in the article were: One, development. Two, protection. Three, it can build confidence. Four, you can find faith. There was a point where I was convinced that once my basketball career was over and I did not have a platform anymore, I wouldn't be able to take over the world like "Pinky and the Brain." Eager to change the world, I wrongly thought that having a sports background was the most effective way to make an impact. Reflecting on it now, I am so pleased that God has watched over me and kept me concealed. Truly, being effective was the real aim, and playing basketball was the most comfortable and appointed area of my life that would allow me to do just that, even though I dreaded being at the forefront. If I had to be in the limelight, I wanted to do it with the one thing that brought me comfort. Now, with writing this book, I still get to do it with the one true thing that is my refuge: God. Today, in my prayer with God, I thanked him for my time in obscurity and asked him to continue to develop me, and when he is no longer keeping me concealed, your girl will be ready to step into the light. My respect for him is now stronger than my fear of being propelled into society's darkness. Or should I say, I am getting to that point? Unfortunately, for the vision that God has placed inside of me, a part of me would love to stay hidden and still be able to execute the plan, but then there is the other side of me that is ready to explore the fullness of God's promises. Then there is the unhinged part of me, the part that you heard about in the stories throughout this book who is deliberately disobedient, feels safer with God even when being mischievous. Let me explain! Merely because of God's grace, mercy, and my knowing that he loves me. Rather than facing the darkness of the world and the people in it who will love you when it's convenient for them and hate you the very next minute. I know God will love me unconditionally, but of course, I am more afraid of him taking his hand off me than facing the cruelness of the world.

TO MY BASKETBALL GIRLIES

In February 2023, I was blessed to be inducted into the Basketball Hall of Fame at my Junior College, Moberly Area Community College. When I first learned about the induction, I felt honored but also triggered because I had experienced shame for most of my life after my career. The shame carried after my basketball career was over, stemmed from me internalizing what I thought the world expected from me. There was also this notion of disappointment and feeling stupid for putting my hopes and dreams into one thing and not diversifying my portfolio. This situation sort of reminds me of the story of the parable of the talents. You know, in the book of **Matthew, Chapter 25 verses 14-30 (ESV)**, when a man went on a journey and entrusted his property to his servants. Scripture says, *"To one he gave five talents of money, to another two talents, and another one talent, each according to his ability. Then he went on his journey."* When he returned, the servants that he gave the five and two talents of money to provide their master with a praiseworthy ROI (return on investment). Which is tenfold, but the one he gave one talent of money to came back with nothing. Scripture says, *"The man with one talent of money dug a hole and buried his master's money."* Now, in some way, I differ from him because I didn't dig a hole and bury my talent of playing basketball. Your girl was for sure dominating the hardwood, but where our similarities lie is that instead of digging a hole and hiding my gift of playing basketball from the world. I hid behind the notion that the game was who I was and not what I did. Putting my identity into something fleeting and being afraid of stepping outside my comfort zone was foolish. I believed it was the best and only thing that would open other doors and help me make my dreams a reality. Instead of banking on basketball, I should have relied on the almighty! This parable is telling God's children that he has given all of us gifts, whether it be 5 or 1, he expects each and everyone of us to be fruitful and multiply, providing light to the world! We all want to hear him say what it says in **Matthew *25:23***

"His master replied, Well done, good and faithful servant! You have been faithful with a few things; I will put you in charge of many things. Come and share your master's happiness." (NIV)

and not what it says in the next couple of verses, when the master spoke to the servant who dug a hole, buried his money and brought nothing back.

"His master replied, You wicked, lazy servant! So, you knew that I harvest where I have not sown and gather where I have not scattered seed? Well then, you should have put my money on deposit with the bankers, so that when I returned, I would have received it back with interest." Matthew 25:26-27 (NIV)

In previous chapters, I shared with you a text message that I sent to my therapist. The message not only spoke about my moments of feeling like the Apostle Paul, but also how I shared the same adversity as Naomi as well. In the Bible, the book of Ruth tells a story of finding favor in the famine. The Bible tells us that Naomi had lost everything. She first lost her home she had known for so long because of the famine in the land, then her husband, and thereafter her two sons. Scripture says that Naomi believed that God's hand had gone out against her.

"Don't call me Naomi," she told them. Call me Mara because the Almighty has made my life very bitter. I went away full, but the Lord has brought me back empty. Why call me Naomi? The Lord has afflicted me; the Almighty has brought misfortune upon me." (Ruth 1:20-21 NIV)

After losing everything, I too, like Naomi, believed that I no longer had anything to offer the world. After every performance-based loss in my life, whether it was basketball rejection, being terminated from a job, or getting dumped by a fiance, the more life rejected me, the more my afflictions grew deeper. The good news is that Naomi endured the long-suffering the Bible speaks about and so can I! Guess what? You will be able to as well despite today's society needing to have everything wrapped in a pretty bow, craving instant gratification. I was burdened by this too, and some days it still lingers. In our walk with the Lord, timing is key, and everything that will happen will come in God's timing. As humans, our brains are finite, but God is omnipresent, omnipotent, and omniscient, so when you have the creator in your corner, patience is critical. Naomi was worried that her time in finding a kinsman redeemer was over because of her being older, but God amid the famine gave her favor. Ultimately, Naomi's bloodline had been redeemed, but in God's timing. This blessing would soon produce the lineage that led to King David and Jesus Christ.

Look at my speech below as I accepted my Hall of Fame award. God has been writing this book for me throughout my life. He has given me the okay to understand some reasons I have been going through all these things thus far. If you take nothing else from this book, absorb these heartfelt words from one beauty to another!

"I would be remiss if I didn't tell you that receiving the news about being inducted into the hall of fame excited me but also triggered me. It has been a while since I had a basketball in my hand and for most of my life, that is all I knew. To where I placed my value in the game and focused solely on the numbers and hype of it all, but when the roars stopped and the curtains closed, I was stuck for a long time! I had to introduce myself to the new me and find that confidence again. I say all of that to say, to the ladies of MACC, if you learn nothing else from me today, learn this. Your worth is not in the game of basketball. Yes, give all you have to it while you are here, but know you are more than enough, and you will do even greater things! To MACC, the board, and the boosters, thank you for this honor. This is truly a great accomplishment. To Coach K, Coach Smith, and my former teammates, thank you for putting up with me. I gave them the blues y'all! To the die-hard Greyhound fans, thank you. To my close family, and friends, to my dad, for your love and support, I am grateful. To my sister, thank you for being loyal and constant in my life. To my

son, thank you for choosing me. You are truly my greatest accomplishment! Most of all, thank you to the one who is my anchor, the one who gave me a newfound gift and confidence in speaking light to myself and others, Jesus Christ, without him I am nothing! Thank you, everyone.

Thanks to you as well! Yep, you! The one who is reading this book. I am grateful you came along with me on this journey to unlock all the lessons and blessings that have made me who I am today. Thank you for taking moments to process, unpack, and release whatever has you happy, anxious, or sad. Remember to continue to seek him for yourself, and when you are having a challenging time finding and remembering who you are in this world, just fixate on the one who created you, Yeshua! If you are having trouble, seeing yourself as God sees you, allow me to give you a little exercise you can implement in the last journal section of the book.

For years, I would say affirmations to myself in the mirror, and although they helped for a moment, the words never stuck to my ribs. After my one conversation with God when he asked me, "**Why are the things I do for you not enough**" and my response was, "**Because I'm not enough.**" It may have been a brief time later when he replied and said, "**Do I live within you?**" My response was "**Yes.**" At that very moment I thought, just take those same affirmations I would say about myself like, "I am beautiful," "I am love," "I am strength," "I am courageous," and put God in the forefront. Then it became, "God is beautiful," "God is love," "God is strength," "God is courageous." BOOM, and there you have it! There is a cheat code to it sticking to your ribs and or your heart. Remember, if our Lord is these things and he lives within us through the

Holy Spirit, therefore these traits are tangible and ready to be received. This allowed me to take the pressure off trying to be perfect and perform, and leave the righteousness to the incredibly good one, God!

"Why do you call me good?" Jesus answered. "No one is good except God alone," (Luke 18:19 NIV)

The one who has already taken the stripes for us, and who is truly these things with no blemishes. He is the one and only true Savior! So, listen here and listen well. Savior, Savior He is, and I am not!

JOURNAL

_____

A MOMENT TO RELEASE

Are you fighting to find your light? If so, what is your deepest fear about stepping into the calling God has for your life? Write and hand your fears over to the Lord, get out everything you would like to say to him, or to those who have wronged you etc. This is your moment to unpack, process, and release any strongholds. In this section, give some examples of what you are currently doing to make this world a better place.

_____ _____

_____

_____

_____

_____

_____

_____

_____

_____

_____

_____

_____

_____

"IT IS FINISHED"

"When he had received the drink, Jesus said, "It is finished." With that, he bowed his head and gave up his spirit."
(John 19:30 NIV)

NOTES

"Parents just don't understand" (DJ Jazzy Jeff & The Fresh Prince, "He's the DJ, I'm the Rapper," 1988)

"Allow me to reintroduce myself" (Jay-Z, "Public Service Announcement Interlude, The Black Album, 2003)

"But what they don't know is when you get home and get behind closed doors, man you hit the floor, and what they can't see is your own your knees" (Mary-Mary, "God in Me" The Sound, 2008)

"Forever, forever, ever forever, ever" (OutKast, "Ms. Jackson," Stankonia, 2000)

"You never know if your light will be the hope for someone else that's all alone" (Victory, "Weatherman" The Broken Instrument, 2018)

ABOUT THE AUTHOR

Mesha was born and raised in Saint Louis, Missouri. Enamored by the women and men of the professional basketball leagues, she set out to become the first woman in the NBA. Along the journey, she struggled to find her identity but was still able to leave an imprint on the court, in the hearts of fans and at her alma mater. Despite not making it to the league, Mesha's athletic accolades still afforded her the honor of being an inductee in the 2023 Basketball Hall of Fame at her junior college, Moberly Area Community College. God has pushed Mesha out of her comfort zone, and into the world of writing and creating. She has always been a dreamer, creating stories in her head, but did not find her gift of writing until her later years. She was the creator and writer for a tall women's blog called "My Height, My Crown," and editor and chief of a Magazine she created called "Hashtag Tall Magazine." Mesha has endured a lot in her days, but by the grace and mercy of her father in heaven, she is starting to rise out of the ashes like a Phoenix and is excited for the next chapter of her life.